Seven Seasons, Seven Lessons

By

Judy Teague R.N.

May the lessons
that each day brings
help you to grow in grace
and knowledge.

Blessings,

Judy

Dedication

To my son, Tyler, he inspired me to take a risk, challenge myself, explore ideas, and to write. When I see Tyler in heaven and he asks me, "what did you do after I left?" I can answer, "I wrote a book." He will look surprised and then smile.

Foreword

I remember the situation like it was yesterday, walking down the hallway into the room of a guy I had just met about an hour ago. I remember feeling embarrassed and awkward to enter the room, but it was something I had promised I would do. Why did I feel that way? I was a volunteer at the hospital. I worked in the playroom on the Oncology floor. My job was to facilitate the playroom. My duties included making rounds to encourage the patients to get out of bed and come play. Usually, when I made the rounds I would stop in, say hi, invite them to the playroom, and leave. But meeting Tyler was completely different. We talked for a long time, and when I realized I needed to get back to what I was doing; instead of saying good-bye for the night I promised to come back later. I knew there was something special about him, and I had to come back to figure it out.

That night in the playroom we painted the patients heads with different designs and they painted our faces. My face turned out to be black with white spots, similar to a backward Dalmatian, and my arms were red. It was pretty interesting, but the patients loved it. After we closed for the night, I made the trek down the hallway to Tyler's room in embarrassment. I had just met the guy and was now walking into his room with paint all over me. What was he going to think of me? How were we going to have a conversation without him laughing the entire time?

As I walked into his room, the embarrassment turned to comfort and acceptance because Tyler let his sense of humor come out right away by making a few jokes. After laughing and explaining the situation, Tyler and I were ready to start one of the most amazing friendships ever. As I left the hospital I realized what a blessing God had put in my life, someone that looked past the "paint" and got to know me for me.

Tyler was someone who loved communication. Many times in the beginning we would talk in his hospital room about anything and everything, usually God, which was amazing. Over time Tyler and I began talking on the phone, hanging out at his house, going to movies, and out to lunch. We had a blast together and the conversations could have gone on for hours, that was Tyler…he loved to talk. We were just what each other needed…I was there to get Tyler out of the house and be a teenager, and Tyler was there to teach me. We also were there to pray for each other, make each other laugh, and make memories together.

Over the course of many times spent together I learned a lot from Tyler. Things I will hold with me for the rest of my life. As I read this book I was reminded of many memories with Tyler, especially the one above. I also reflected on what Tyler taught me. What stuck out the most was his honesty. Tyler knew who he was and was confident with the person God had shaped him to be. He was in the midst of a battle, and day in and day out faced it head on. He fought to the best of his ability, and when he needed help he expressed it. That's what I loved about him. He was courageous, but at the same time not afraid to admit his need for help, whether that was to adjust his pillow, talk on the phone, or to get him out of the house.

One day in particular Tyler's honesty absolutely amazed me. I was at the mall when he called to tell me the update about his treatment. Unfortunately it wasn't good, there was no longer a way to eliminate the cancer, the only option was palliative treatment. Tyler informed me of the news and what was to come, and thanked me for all that we had shared together. You would expect it to be one of the most terrible things to hear, and it pretty much was, but for some reason it was ok. He was honest about who he was, what he was fighting, and now where he was going. He truly amazed me; in the midst of such sadness Tyler smiled and made it ok. He continued to fight and we continued our friendship; we talked and laughed together, we made memories together, we were teenagers together.

Throughout his treatment Tyler was honest with God, himself, his family, and his friends. His honesty encouraged me to look inward and really get to know who I was and who God wanted me to be. Because of our friendship, I have done just that and found it one of the most rewarding things. I continue to live out the valuable lessons Tyler taught me. Some are harder than others, but I know that no matter what life brings I can get through it, by fixing my eyes on Christ and putting one hundred percent faith in God. There are times when I think the pain hurts too much or the situation won't ever come to a happy end, but it is in those times that I am reminded of my good friend, Tyler. Tyler never gave up, he fought his heart out, and when necessary, he called for help.

For those of you who were also blessed to know Tyler, I would encourage you to reflect on Tyler's friendship in your life. Take time to think about the memories you made together, the things he taught you, and don't forget to laugh, after all that's probably what Tyler would have done. For those of you who never knew Tyler personally, he truly was everything this book expresses him as and more. Spend time reflecting on the different lessons and how you can apply them to your life.

To Tyler...thank you for your lessons, your love, and your friendship. You are in my heart forever and always, I love you and miss you!

Dawn Green

INTRODUCTION

"Give sorrow words: the grief that does not speak, whispers the over-wrought heart and bids it break." Shakespeare in Macbeth

My decision to write this book involved many considerations. During Tyler's treatment, I faithfully kept a journal. Tyler's treatment lasted 574 very long days; each day I wrote a short note of thoughts, verses, and things Tyler said or did. I included words of encouragement that we received from visitors, calls, cards, and email. I also included the treatment that Tyler had to endure each day. So I had an accurate account of Tyler's battle with this terrible disease.

Writing this journal was valuable in helping me to cope with this unbearable situation, but after the journal ended, I did not want to just put it away in a drawer. I felt a need to use it in some way to honor Tyler.

Grief counselors will tell you that writing can be very helpful in dealing with the burden of grief. I have seen that several families from the 9-11 tragedy have written books about their loved ones. I pray that these families find comfort in telling about their loved ones. I, too, am seeking to find a measure of comfort by telling Tyler's story. So after much time dwelling on format, what to say and how to say it one day I decided to quit thinking about it and "just do it."

I did have one major obstacle to overcome; my writing ability could be compared to Moses' speaking ability. So following Moses' example of having his brother, Aaron speak for him: I ask Tyler's brother, Travis to help by editing this short book. Also, I knew that if I wrote the book alone, and Tyler was here, he would say, "Mom, you wrote a 'girl' book!" So I am grateful to Travis for his willingness to help and for his male perspective.

Another consideration in my decision to write about Tyler's story is out of a sense to duty. Warren Wiersbe said, "I cannot keep my privileges for myself, I must use them for others." He explains further that "If you want to find out what a worker is really like, don't give him *responsibilities,* give him *privileges."*

Tyler was a blessing to us; we were blessed with this *privilege* for almost 19 years. But now it is time to take the *responsibility* and, in some small way, to give back what we were given from Tyler's short life.

When a loved one dies, there is a tendency to 'enshrine' him, which is to remember only the good things about the loved one and to ignore any faults. Tyler, of course, had his faults; which Travis can verify. And Tyler would be the first to admit his faults and shortcomings and even joke about them. This just made you love him even more.

But the purpose of this writing is to give positive lessons from Tyler's life, so we have emphasized Tyler's good qualities and mini-mized his faults. So please forgive our one-sided viewpoint. Some of the lessons overlap, and some things may be repeated; we hope that this will emphasize the thought and not be redundant. We hope that from this short book, you can find something good, one lesson to apply, or at least, a thought to consider.

Seven Lessons, Seven Days

Why seven lessons? In the Bible, the number seven is the number of completeness or perfection. The Bible begins with seven days of creation, and in Revelation, there are seven churches and seven seals. And the number seven is used throughout scripture.

Now, by no means, am I implying that these seven lessons will make anyone complete or perfect, I simply liked the symbolism of the number. I like to think that although Tyler's life was short, it was complete.

Tyler fought his battle for seven seasons. To give my readers a clearer picture of Tyler's physical battle and his indomitable response to it, I have included a summary of one season after each lesson. Drawing from my journal and Ken's informative and descriptive updates on Tyler's website, I give a brief synopsis of each of the seven seasons. And to close each lesson I share a small sample of the over 1,200 messages and cards that Tyler received. So for seven days, I would ask you to place this writing by your bed and read one lesson each morning or evening.

"From everyone who has been given much, much will be demanded; and from the one who had been entrusted with much, much more will be asked." Luke 12:48

LESSON 1

FOUNDATION

"We are not human beings trying to be spiritual. We are spiritual beings trying to be human." Jacquelyn Small

Tyler was born on July 9, 1985 in Humble Texas. His dad, Ken, was a chemical engineer and his mom, Judy, was an RN. He had one older brother, Travis who was four and a half years old. He began his physical journey strong and healthy. He was blessed with a family that loved him and was able to provide a nice middle-class home for him (that means that he didn't have to share a room with his brother). He had a happy childhood while moving around Texas, Denver, Calgary, and California. He quickly made friends everytime we moved and enjoyed spending time with them but was also happy to spend time alone.

I think the best word to describe Tyler as he grew up was content. He was happy with what he had and didn't complain about what he didn't have. Why was he content? The fact that he was loved and provided for physically was an important part. But more importantly, a trust in God was the foundation for his contentment. As

Tyler grew physically, his inquisitive mind developed. Sometime in his early childhood, he began to believe in God. As he matured, this belief expanded to trust in God.

His spiritual journey began in the most ordinary way, through Bible stories, songs, and prayers. Our family attended services each Sunday and Wednesday throughout Tyler's childhood. He was always eager to learn about God's word. He was a good listener, and about the age of 10 I realized through his remarks afterward that he usually learned more from each service than I did. As he grew physically, he also grew in grace and knowledge, through personal Bible study, Bible classes, sermons, prayer and discussions. This was Tyler's "basic training" to lay a foundation for his life. So as a child and teen Tyler had a basic knowledge of the scriptures, the scriptures that can make you wise for salvation through faith in Jesus (read 2 Tim. 3:14-17).

Tyler built his life on the foundation of the Word of God and anchored his hope by complete trust in God. To state the obvious, any building project needs a strong foundation. Tyler had a good foundation to begin building his life.

God reveals that Jesus is the cornerstone of this foundation. The prophet Isaiah wrote, *"See, I lay a stone in Zion, a tested stone, a precious cornerstone for a sure foundation; the one who trusts will never be dismayed"* (Isaiah 28:16). So many years before Jesus came to earth as a physical man God revealed that he had prepared for us a cornerstone.

Tyler also had an anchor. We need the anchor of hope to secure our soul through our physical journey. The Bible says, *"We have this hope to secure as an anchor for the soul, firm and secure"* (Heb. 6:19). We are spiritual beings on a physical journey. God gives us the analogy of a cornerstone and an anchor to explain that He is with us on this journey.

We are spiritual beings on a physical journey. We are human.

We have a physical body. C. S. Lewis said, " *God never meant man to be a purely spiritual creature. That is why He uses material things like bread and wine to put new life into us.*" So let's switch gears and talk about the foundation we need to build for our physical lives, the lives that we wake up to each day.

Although Tyler was an easy-going kid, he set high expectations for himself. He took the day-to-day ups and downs all in stride. And this attitude worked well for him. He liked to compare life to the video games that he loved to play. One of his favorite games was the role-playing game, Final Fantasy X. In this game, each object obtained or lesson learned could be used later in a critical place or time.

He also applied this game strategy to other areas of his life. Tyler's dream was to go to the Naval Academy and become an officer in the Marines. When he was a Freshman at Stockdale High School, in Bakersfield, California, he began steps to make this dream a reality.

Travis was now in his first year at Cal Poly in San Luis Obispo. Tyler had learned from his brother that you need to prepare, plan and purpose to make dreams real. So to prepare himself for the military lifestyle, in March of 2000, he joined the Bakersfield Young Marines and later that year transferred to the Saddleback Young Marines in Orange County.

Tyler loved being a Young Marine. Being a Young Marine gave him the perfect opportunity to learn that once you have the right foundation you can turn problems into challenging games with solutions rather than burdens to carry around. Tyler quickly realized that once you apply yourself to learn the rules and principles and make it through "basic training," you can then strategically build and grow in the Young Marines or in life itself.

Now the point of this lesson is not that every teenager needs to go join the Young Marines. The military basis of this organization is certainly not for everyone. But the point is to *be engaged in life.* The opportunities to be involved in life are endless: be a part of some group, organization, or club. You will learn lessons about life, build social skills, increase your emotional intelligence, and meet people. This can also be done through a job, sports, or volunteer work.

Tyler was in the high school marching band at both high schools he attended and at New Mexico Military Institute (NMMI) for the short time that he attended there. Tyler played the saxophone in both marching and concert bands. This experience also provided Tyler a foundation to build upon. Being a part of the Stockdale band in Bakersfield, the Aliso Niguel band in Orange County and the NMMI band in Roswell gave Tyler another opportunity to learn that life is a building project.

Once again, we are spiritual beings on a physical journey. We need a spiritual foundation, a trust in God; and a physical foundation, built through being engaged in life.

So the first and most critical lesson from Tyler is to build on the right foundation and to anchor your life through hope and trust in God. When the storms of life come into any part of your life, social, spiritual, school, physical, or other, it is the foundation that will hold or fall, and the anchor will secure or fail. Once you have the cornerstone set in your foundation and a firm anchor secured, it is possible to build a life that can withstand the storms, trials, and burdens that will come. And I can testify that they WILL COME!

These storms might be a small windstorm, perhaps a bad grade on a homework assignment; or a medium size tornado, maybe a rejection from your first choice of a university; or the storm might be a class 5 hurricane, a diagnosis of a rare and aggressive cancer.

In the summer of 2002, Tyler had worked very hard to finish high school a year early. In August he had began his first semester at New Mexico Military Institute (NMMI) in Roswell. NMMI is a prep school for all the Military Academies. He hoped to be accepted into the Naval Academy the following year. So everything was falling into place. As Tyler would put it, he was, "Good to go."

But Tyler's foundation would soon be tested. In October, he became very constipated while visiting his Uncle Jerry and Aunt Arlene in Texas. Tyler was 17 years old and appeared to be a picture of health. But after three weeks and several tests later, the doctors determined that Tyler needed immediate surgery.

On November 1st during a six-hour surgery they removed a 10-pound tumor near his rectum. They said that it was malignant and had already metastasized to his liver and abdominal area. The surgeon tried to tell us this devastating news as kindly as she could. She said, "It's OK to be sad."

In the recovery room, we told Tyler that he had cancer. He cried a few tears and said, "I can't be a Marine." Tyler was 17 years old and facing a storm that would test his foundation in ways that he never expected. He was suppose to be a Marine, not a cancer patient. He was suppose to meet his enemy on the battlefield, not in the hospital. This was not the battle he wanted. But it was the one that he was given, and he faced it with the same attitude that he did everything else. Trust in God.

Paul wrote to Timothy, *"Endure hardship with us like a good soldier of Jesus Christ"* (2 Tim. 2:3). Tyler's wonderful friend, Lindsey had given him the nickname Soldier Boy because of his love for the military. He liked that nickname. Tyler was a soldier facing a formidable enemy. To watch Tyler endure his treatment day in and day out was truly a lesson in being a good soldier. It was a combination of spiritual "basic training" and physical "basic training" that gave him the right foundation and secure anchor that he needed for his storm.

"When the storm has swept by, the wicked are gone, but the righteous stand firm forever," Proverbs 10:25

APPLICATION FOR LESSON #1 FOUNDATION

Key principles: Build your life on the right foundation.
Hope and trust in God.
Use the true anchor, Jesus Christ.
Be engaged in life.

Verse to remember: Hebrews 6:19

Psalm to read: Psalm 25

Words to study: foundation, anchor, trust

Websites to visit: *www.biblegateway.com*
www.youngmarines.com
www.nmmi.edu

Recommended book: Mere Christianity by C. S. Lewis

Something to do today: Go for a walk, think about what is the foundation of your life.
What are the lessons from your life?

Fall 2002 Season of Shock and Awe

In the fall of 2002, Ken and I were just beginning to adjust to our empty nest. Ken was a project engineer for ARB, a pipeline construction company. I was working at an outpatient surgery center. Travis was pursuing plans to go to law school and Tyler was on track to becoming an officer in the Marines. We missed the boys but were proud of their accomplishments. Life was good. But that fall our lives would be changed forever, by a diagnosis we had never heard of.

Tyler was diagnosed with desmoplastic small round cell tumor. DSRCT was first described in medical literature in 1991. It is a very rare and aggressive cancer. It is predominately found in teens and young adults. It is found in males more than females. It usually originates in the abdomen or pelvis. Prognosis is very poor and survival rates are not possible to define. Treatment is based on the individual case. I left my nursing job to be Tyler's primary caregiver. As a surgical nurse I had no experience in oncology or home health, but I soon was engaged in a personal and hands-on crash course.

Tyler was to receive his treatment at Children's Hospital of Orange County (CHOC). Tyler's initial treatment protocol was surgery to debulk the tumor, followed by seven rounds of high dose chemotherapy, followed by a stem cell transplant and radiotherapy. The treatment would take 10-12 months. The odds were against Tyler; but Tyler was Soldier Boy. He was armed with his faith and military attitude. He said, "Well, I have a problem; let's fix it and move on." He had lessons to teach.

Fall 2002 Messages to Tyler

Tyler
Andy Anderson December 12, 2002

I mentioned this to your folks, but I also want to express to you my admiration for your faith and courage. What a splendid example your are demonstrating to everyone who knows you! Hang in there!
Andy Anderson

Sending you a hug from Hart, TX
Marie Clevenger December 15, 2002

Hello Tyler,
What a great way to stay in touch with you and have updates on your recovery. We miss seeing your smiling face. You are very much in our prayers and thoughts. Many, many people are caring for you and loving you though this rough time.
Love in Christ,
Marie and Duane Clevenger

For Cryin' out loud!
Jb Emery December 16, 2002

I'm glad I'm not your Pop! I've never seen a fella get so many ladies to leave messages! Your Dad better keep a good swingin' stick near by to keep them at bay. Hey holler at me when you feel you can put up with me for a couple of mins. I've got a 13th MEU (SOC) unit coin with your name on it. Keep your mind sharp and your soul strong.
Love ya and God Bless "jb" Emery

Hello Tyler
Steven Cody December 16, 2002
Hi Tyler,

My name is Steve Cody and I am a business associate/ friend of your father's. Although we have never met, Ken has told me all about you. You sound like a fine young man, and your father is very proud of you and loves you very much as I'm sure you know.

I want you to know that me, my wife Mary, and our whole church (River Oaks Church in Bakersfield) are all praying for your comfort and healing. I know that with God's help and the support of your friends and family, you will get better. Keep the faith!

Best wishes,
Steve Cody

Wow Tyler
Leslie Flad December 18, 2002
It's so awesome to come here for an update and see that you have so many friends :) !! God is awesome. We are continually praying for you and your strength. I know that when I had cancer, the strength of the brethren and the kind encouragement got me through, so here I am to tell you again, keep the faith, hang in there and don't loose sight of your goal. The brethren are faithful, and prayer is awesome. We love you. In Him, the Flads

Advice from Your TC
Chris Priebe December 18, 2002
Well big guy, looks like you're still doing better than anyone expected, so keep up the fight. I'm still gonna work on convincing you to give up the Marine Corps and see the Army light, and personally I think that'll be a much harder fight. Just remember, no matter the odds, or apathy - One with the Lord is a majority. Looking at all the people here with you, praying for you - you'll

come out ok. You always manage to anyway. I remember how you could do things here and "vanish" so you couldn't get punished....in plain site too, do something entirely insane, and then just not be noticed...You've gotten outa tight situations before, You'll make it again.

Chris Priebe

Headquarters Troop Commander

NMMI

Hello from Finals Week!!!

Rebeccah Todd December 18, 2002

Hey Tyler,

What's crackin? We just got the info for this site yesterday. I hope you know that we all miss having you around and that it has never truly been the same here without you. It's good to know that you're still the court jester. Everybody has been working really hard lately for finals so we can come back next semester. Well, all I wanted to say is that we miss you and that everybody's praying for you to get well.

Rat Buddies for Life,

Becca Todd

(((((((((((((((((Tyler))))))))))))))))) (big hug).

Kenda Morgan December 23, 2002

Hi! I am sooo happy that you insisted on being home for Christmas! That's the best medicine. Tyler, my acquaintance with you was also during an earlier phase when you guys were moving around the country for your dad's work and I am sure you don't remember a lot of those connections from when you were small. But your personality made a distinct impression on me when we both lived in Colorado as a very active, sociable, affable member of your family. I was very sorry to hear of your being sick and also for the aggression of your treatment, in order to be even meaner to the cancer. It feels like there is a zero-to-sixty quality to jumping into this treatment for your illness that has to have been shocking to you and your folks. Knowing your family, you guys are managing this tangent in your lives as well as anyone could, already. But, you can be sure that the messages you have been getting are the tip of the iceberg.... they represent a lot more people out here sending out their constant, best wishes for your health.

Your friend,

Kenda

LESSON 2

EDUCATION

"Wonder is the beginning of wisdom." Greek proverb

Tyler loved to learn; his mind was full of questions. He was curious about almost any subject; and he wanted to educate himself about everything from atoms and molecules to astronomy. The second lesson from Tyler is educate yourself.

While this certainly applies to a formal education of high school and college, Tyler's lesson is about the other kind of education. The education of learning about life through books, TV programs, movies, music, friends and daily life. Tyler loved books, next to a good movie his favorite place to go was the bookstore. Read not only for school and work, but also for your own education. Reading is the gateway to exploring and learning. Reading gives us experiences that otherwise we would never know. Read the Bible, 2 Tim.2:15 says, *"Be diligent to present yourself approved to God, a worker who does not need to be ashamed, rightly dividing the word of truth."* Diligent means *constant and earnest in effort and application*. I like that definition, be diligent! Educate yourself.

Read fiction. Tyler loved the series, Brotherhood of War, by W.E.B. Griffin. Read non-fiction. Tyler enjoyed political books like Bill O'Reilly's, Who's Looking Out for You? Read about history. Black Hawk Down by Mark Bowden and The Killer Angels by Michael Shaare were two of Tyler's favorite books about history. Read literature. Tyler's favorite book he read for school was The Things They Carried, by Tim O'Brien.

Tyler educated himself in unconventional ways; he loved watching the Simpsons. Yes, I know, a lot of parents won't even let their kids watch this program and I certainly respect their concerns. I realize that to put this in the lesson on education is a stretch; but I could not write a book about Tyler and not mention the Simpsons. Tyler loved to watch and find the deeper meaning of each episode. Again, I know that some of you question, isn't using the Simpson's and deeper meaning in the same sentence an oxymoron? Perhaps. Matt Groening, the creator of the Simpsons says, "The Simpsons is a show that rewards you for paying attention." The Simpsons is written with allusion, parody, irony and satire. We laugh at the Simpsons because we see ourselves in them. From this viewpoint we can learn more about ourselves.

In the episode, Homer vs. Lisa and the 8th commandment, Homer gets an illegal cable TV hookup and invites all his friends to the house to watch a major boxing match. Lisa learns about the 8th commandment at Sunday school and fears her family will go to hell for stealing cable. She seeks the advice of the preacher, who tells her to set an example by not watching any cable programs. Marge also worries that the cable is a negative influence on her family and wants to get rid of it. On the night of the big boxing match, Lisa protests and is sent outside by Homer, where Marge joins her. But during the fight, Homer's conscience finally wins over and he joins his family. Afterwards, Homer climbs the power pole and cuts the cable line, plunging the neighborhood into darkness, from the book,

The Simpsons, a complete guide to our favorite family. If you use your imagination, you could use this episode to talk about several lessons, the 8th commandment, stealing, the other commandments, Lisa teaching Homer about honesty and Homer finally admitting that he was wrong.

Tyler could write a book about the Simpsons, but I hope that I have made the point that lessons can be learned through unconventional sources and that even a silly show like the Simpsons can lead to educational discussions. Tyler knew that learning could be fun.

Tyler's other favorite program was the exact opposite of the Simpsons, the History Channel, or as we preferred to call it "the War Channel." Tyler's memory for facts he heard on television, especially the History Channel, was amazing. His love of military history along with his recall of these programs gave him a knowledge and the capacity to have a discussion with anyone who was also interested in this subject.

Some may ask, what's so important about history? Rarely is History the favorite subject of students. Some may find history interesting but don't really find it useful. I found the importance of history summed up in six words. David McCullough, the Pulitzer Prize winning author of many books including John Adams, said, *"knowledge of history leads to gratitude."* That statement was an epiphany for me. There have probably been several books written about the importance to history, but to condense it down to six words was enlightening. I would like to apply this thought that knowledge of history leads to gratitude in three ways.

Tyler enjoyed learning about history, especially U. S. History, specifically the war history of our country. He knew the history of the Marines from their beginning on July 11, 1798 to today. Tyler was very grateful to be an American; he was proud and patriotic. He loved his country and wanted to serve his country. He knew that to understand the true value of freedom, you need to know the price that was paid. A history lesson in the cost of freedom is a lesson on gratitude. The Civil War chaplain, Abram Joseph Ryan said, *"a land without ruins is a land without memories, a land without memories is a land without history."* Nations must bear conflict and suffering, as citizens we must be grateful enough to know our history.

Another area of history leading to gratitude to consider is the history of your personal life. Our memories of the families that nurtured us, the friends that loved us, teachers that inspired us, and trials that we endured can increase our gratitude and appreciation for our own lives. Lewis Smedes said, *"A person who had the habit of hope also has the habit of remembering. Hope needs memories, happy memories of fulfilled dreams, grateful memories of bad things we survived."*

Memories, remembering, who has the time and energy for all this self-introspection and soul-searching? As Alexander Chase said, *"memory is the thing that you forget with."* So the best solution is to write it down. Keep a journal; write down your history.

I found, during Tyler's illness, that writing gave me a way to cope, a way to reduce stress, and a way to memorialize our story. Writing was my therapy. Studies show that people who write 20 minutes a day about traumatic events improve their immune systems, reduce doctor's visits and use less medication. I think that this is especially helpful to those of us that are not comfortable talking about ourselves or are less articulate than we would like to be.

To go back now and read my journal is difficult, but helpful. Recalling Tyler's attitude helps me remember his smile; reading about the many visits and calls from friends helps me remember the blessings of brotherly love; to read the verses I wrote in searching for comfort reminds me that in spite of it all, there is a God. I could not do this if I had not written it down. God created time; he made the days and nights, the seasons, the years. A journal is a history of your journey through seasons of joy, grief, achievements and gratitude.

One third and final thought about history leading to gratitude, I transfer to a spiritual realm. In over 3,100 years of recorded history, only 286 of those years were warless. Humanity has endured these many years of war, but there has also been a spiritual war recorded. *"Crowns of roses fade, but crowns of thorns endure,"* wrote Abram Joseph Ryan. The climax of this spiritual war is recorded in the historical books of Matthew, Mark, Luke and John. These books record the words, works, miracles, crucifixion and resurrection of our Lord and Savior. This history lesson is the foundation for our salvation. We give glory to God with a grateful heart.

Now I will move on to a lighter subject and one of Tyler's favorites, movies. Tyler loved going to movies with friends and his family, especially his Uncle Rick. During his treatment, Tyler was unable to do a lot of activities that he previously enjoyed, but we were fortunate that when he was home, he usually felt well enough to go to a movie. Not only did Tyler watch the movie but also he enjoyed critiquing it by finding any subplots, doing character analysis and remembering specific quotes. Tyler saw movies as another way to educate himself.

In the fall of 2000, Tyler was a pleasant and cheerful teenager. Yes, teenagers can be pleasant and cheerful. Tyler was the picture of health; he was active as a drill instructor in the Young Marines, played saxophone in the marching band and was making A's and B's in school. One afternoon I came home and he was watching the movie Stripes with Bill Murry. But he wasn't just watching the movie, he had recorded a particular scene where Bill Murry's character is doing a rifle routine and Tyler was replaying this scene over and over while he had his own rifle and was learning the routine himself. Tyler had taken an amusing and entertaining scene from a 2-star movie and used it to learn something. What did he gain from this? Perhaps nothing more than a little physical exercise, but as he entertained me with his military rifle routine, with his perfect posture and Marine stare, I learned that each day has moments to treasure and he gave me a precious memory.

On December 9th 2003, the day before Tyler was to begin his stem cell transplant; he was recovering from a horrible case of the shingles, a very painful viral infection. The shingles had delayed his transplant for 2 weeks; but on December 9th we were hopeful that he was back on track for a cure that the transplant would bring. Knowing that he would be quarantined in a hospital room for the next 4-6 weeks, Tyler wanted to see a movie, he chose The Last Samurai. After the movie, we went to the park near our house. It was a beautiful, sunny day in Orange County. I made some pictures of Tyler and we talked about the movie. Tyler said that he liked the movie because it was about honor and courage. Tyler's life was also about honor and courage.

Music and radio were important to Tyler, primarily for entertainment, but also for education. We made many trips to the hospital and clinic from our house. The drive usually took about 25 minutes. This was just enough time to listen to one segment on NPR (national public radio). I don't think many teenagers listen to NPR, but Tyler liked learning about the liberal point of view on various topics. It helped balance out the conservative view he heard at home.

Tyler had an extensive CD collection; he always took several with him to the hospital. Some of his favorite groups were U2, Counting Crows, and Red Hot Chili Peppers. He liked to find favorite lyrics and apply them to himself. I always let Tyler pick out what we would listen to on those drives to his treatment. Sometimes Tyler would want to talk about the music or the subject on NPR, and at times he just wanted to be alone in his thoughts. I let him decide. Tyler taught me that sometimes people need someone to talk to and sometimes they just need you to be there.

The Bible has a lot to say about learning, knowledge and

discerning. Let's start at the beginning; Proverbs 1:7 says, *"The fear of the Lord is the beginning of knowledge, but fools despise wisdom and discipline."* The foundation of knowledge is to fear God, to respect and trust God that he is in control. This respect is the key to your knowledge becoming wisdom. Proverbs 23:12 says, *"Apply your heart to instruction and your ears to words of knowledge."* The verse says heart and ears, not mouth. So, if you want to gain knowledge, listen.

Tyler certainly enjoyed expressing his opinion, but he was also a good listener. The next step after listening is discernment. To discern is to show good judgement and understanding. Proverbs 15:14 says, *"The discerning heart seeks knowledge, but the mouth of the fool feeds on folly."* Note the two groups of three words: discern-heart-knowledge or mouth-fool-folly. I like to keep things simple, so to summarize:

Fear God-gain knowledge
Listen-gain knowledge
Discern-gain knowledge

Let's go to the next step. Proverbs 17:27 says, *"A man of knowledge uses words with restraint, and a man of understanding is even-tempered."* Words must be spoken with knowledge, restraint and in a calm manner. So listen to learn then speak with respect, restraint and calmness. That leads to lesson # 3, communication.

"Teach us to number our days, that we may apply our hearts to wisdom." Psalm 90:12

APPLICATION FOR LESSON 2 EDUCATION

Key principle: Educate yourself, be an informed citizen

Verse to remember: 2 Peter 3:18

Psalm to read: Psalm 37

Words to study: knowledge, learn, discern

Websites to visit: www.besthistorysites.com
www.yourDictionary.com

Recommended book: Life's Greatest Lessons, 20 Things That Matter by Hal Urban

Something to do today: Write down your goals, dreams and lessons of your life.

Winter 2003 Season of Preparation

As fall turned to winter our shock and disbelief turned to preparation. We were facing a formidable trial; we had to look past the shock of the diagnosis. The two priorities were to finish seven rounds of chemo and harvest stem cells for the transplant. We were also learning to deal with the day-to-day tasks of flushing the IV catheter with Heparin, colostomy care, drawing blood for lab work, injections to rebuild white blood cells and hemoglobin, pain management, and controlling nausea. We had a good team to deal with all these tasks and we adjusted to our new routine as best we could. Our church family helped with anything we needed and did their best to keep Tyler's weight up by providing delicious home-cooked meals.

Tyler's protocol was to start another round of chemo every 21 days, but because his platelets were always slow to recover the next round was usually delayed. He suffered side effects of leg pain, nausea and terrible mouth and GI tract sores.

Tyler finished his 3rd round of chemo on December 29th and the CT scan done the next day showed that the cancer was responding to the chemo. It was a good note to end the year on. In February, the stem cells were harvested, a process that took three sessions to complete.

It was a difficult winter but by the end of it Tyler had completed five rounds of chemo and his stem cells were stored. We allowed ourselves to feel some hope and optimism.

Winter 2003 Messages to Tyler

Thinking of You
Rick Lopez December 30, 2002

Tyler:

I have put you on our prayer list at Santa Paula Church of Christ. Everyone is very concerned about you. I think of you every day and I know God is putting his healing hand on you. I enjoyed our talk on Christmas Eve and pray that God will keep you and your parents in his loving arms during this whole time.

I love you.

Rick

Thinking About You Often
Mark, Tammy, Kelsie McCoy December 30, 2002

Hi Tyler. Getting the updates on your situation is helpful. I thank God you are home now and your appetite is working. Just a short note to let you know I think about you often and when I do, I go to my Father who controls the universe. I ask Him for many things on your behalf and on your family's. I hope your vision allows you to read His word. If not, ask someone to read I Cor. 8:6 to you. God blesses!!

Mark.

Greetings from Roswell
Jason Moore January 13, 2003

All is well here in the Alien City, and at the church. We pray for you and consider you often. We stand in unison with the countless number of people and congregations who are cheering you on. Your brothers at NMMI are among your biggest fans, and send their greetings, also :>) The Lord bless you, Tyler.

Peace,

Your Church family in Roswell

Greetings from Saudi Arabia

Jim Breninger January 18, 2003

Tyler

Yes, you are getting a message all the way from Saudi Arabia!! Probably sets the distance record for your long list of messages. I read through your updates and while I am still in shock about it all I do have faith that you will continue to get through this and back to college. I have to say I am impressed with your strength and courage but would expect nothing less.

The church family here in Saudi will be praying for you, as will Jill and myself, knowing that God will bless you and care for you.

With all our love,

Jim, Jill & Joel Breninger

ARB support

Amy Thorne January 31, 2003

Hi Tyler,

It's Amy from your dad's work... we've never met, but I've been keeping up with your progress through your website and conversations with your dad. You are in my thoughts and prayers and there are many, many people here at the office who are praying for you and wishing you the best. Stay strong and keep believing. From what I've seen in the other messages that have been posted, you are truly blessed with such a loving family and wonderful friends.

God bless,

Amy Thorne

God bless you
Jana Brooke February 08, 2003

Dear Tyler, Ken, and Judy,

I hope that Tyler is feeling well after his blood transfusion. I am thankful that the sores did not come. I found it interesting that you have to mobilize the stem cells. It is a fitting analogy of getting ready for battle. I am confident that the stem cells will do their job and defeat the cancer. I think about you daily. Look to God when you are feeling low and know that many, many Christians are praying for you.

Love,

Aunt Jana

Good Luck Tomorrow
Bridget Slanaker February 12, 2003

Tyler- Good luck tomorrow with your stem cell collection. Can they pipe in a six-hour Simpson Marathon to pass the time? It's a good thing you can watch movies-I hope you can do it during the collection. I will pray that the time passes quickly so that you can be home in no time. Bridget

Young Marines CO
Nicholas Loskutoff February 27, 2003

Hey Trooper:

I see you are making it through those kimo drills. Must be that Marine attitude of "no pain, no gain" we instilled in you. Hang in there. You are making it to the top of this crucible. As for us, we are doing fine. Had a drill campout last week. This week is the Parade, and next week is a flag ceremony. We are anxiously waiting your return so that you can get back to helping the troops do it correctly.

See you soon

Mr. "L"

LESSON 3

COMMUNICATION

"Be a good talker, be a better listener." Larry King

Tyler was a gifted communicator. He wasn't born that way. At the age of three Tyler still wasn't talking. I vividly remember asking him one day, what is your name? And can you say your name? He just answered "huh." His hearing had been checked and was fine. So I took him to a testing center. After several tests, their results were, "Well he's not stupid!" So with the "not stupid" diagnosis we just let things take their course and about two years later Tyler started talking in complete sentences. A few years after that, he began using and enjoying his gift of communication. Tyler also enjoyed vocabulary, he liked to know the origin of the word and explore the meaning beyond just the first listing in the dictionary. So using Tyler's example I have included some words to study with each of his seven lessons. These are commonly used words that everyone knows the meaning; but words, that if, looked up not only in the dictionary, but also a Bible dictionary, concordance, and thesaurus can give insight and knowledge. That is the foundation of good communication.

One of Tyler's favorite things to do was to have a discussion. He would discuss a wide range of topics. Theology, religion, history, war, the military, philosophy, politics, movies, the Simpsons, and teen social concerns were some of his favorite topics. Not only did Tyler enjoy a wide range of topics but also a wide range of who he had the discussions with, all ages, nationalities, educational levels, men, women, children, Democrats, Republicans, Independents. Tyler enjoyed discussions with his school and Bible class teachers, in fact, he would much rather discuss the homework or assignment than do the homework or assignment.

During his treatment, I was amused and proud, that often I would come into his hospital room and would find him talking to his nurse, for that shift, about various topics. Tyler talked with them about who they should vote for or which church they went to and why. But the thing I found most interesting was how many times they would ask Tyler a question about what they should do about their own teens. Tyler usually had an answer for them. His answer was generally practical, fair, and just common sense. During one of these conversations, he said, "It's better for parents to be too strict than too lenient, because it is easier for kids to forgive their parents than it is to forgive themselves."

So lesson 3 from Tyler is to talk to people about life, ideas, theories, and their hopes and dreams. This lesson has some guide-lines or rules. The Bible says, *"Do not let any unwholesome talk come out of your mouths, but only what is helpful for building others up according to their needs, that it may benefit those who listen"* (Eph. 4:29). Along with the Golden Rule in Matt.7:12, this is one of the most valuable verses to guide us in our relationships with others. So with this verse as our standard, we have four rules to follow when talking to others.

Rule #1 *"Don't let any unwholesome talk come out of your mouth,"*

Don't lie, use profanity, crude humor, put others down or gossip. This rule is the most obvious but often the hardest to follow. It is sometimes just so hard to resist listening to or repeating gossip. Thomas Jefferson said, *"honesty is the first chapter of the book of wisdom."* And Calvin Coolidge said, *"I have never been hurt by anything I didn't say."* In his book, Life's Greatest Lessons, Hal Urban explains that dishonest habits become roadblocks to our growth and development, but that honesty had a built-in reward: a peace of mind, an inner peace.

Rule #2 *"but only what is helpful for building others up"*

To be helpful is to save, rescue, contribute, promote, give aid, assist, and be of service. Help is a small but meaningful word; Webster's lists 22 definitions. So there are endless ways to be helpful. To be helpful in our communication we must "build others up." To build is to develop, increase or strengthen. Some versions use the word to edify. Edify means to build up and encourage morally and spiritually. Practice building others up, affirm them, look for something good to say. Charles Fillmore said, *"We increase what we praise."*

Rule #3 *"according to their needs"*

To fill another person's needs through our words and conversations requires a combination of common sense, empathy and again honesty. The Bible says, *"A word aptly spoken is like apples of gold in settings of silver"* (Proverbs 25:11). What a beautiful description of the right word at the right time! Another verse from Proverbs says, *"A man finds joy in giving an apt reply and how good is a timely word"* (Proverbs 15:23). Both these proverbs use the word apt or aptly. Apt means suited to the purpose or occasion, to the point, appropriate, or relevant. I like that short word, apt.

Rule #4 *"that it may benefit those that listen."*

I think that this would have been Tyler's favorite rule. He took a measure of pride in being able to communicate his ideas and thoughts, in ways that gave himself and others something to think about. It should be a win-win situation, everyone should gain something from the conversation. Joseph Joubut said, *"The aim of an argument or discussion should not be about victory, but progress."*

Tyler loved to have a win-win conversation. And during his treatment he was able to have many win-win conversations. Tyler was blessed to have many visitors during his treatment. This gave him the perfect opportunity to teach and learn about communication. James Thurber said, *"It is better to ask some of the questions than to know all the answers."* That is a good guideline to having a win-win conversation. Ask questions. Find out their opinion and try to understand their point of view. Ask meaningful questions, ask about their hopes and dreams, or thoughts on a verse or quote. Instead of asking, "how is your day going?" ask, "what is something good about today?" We don't know what will happen tomorrow. Make your words of today gracious.

Communication is also about the written word. The written word can edify and affirm. Through the web site www.carepage.com we found a wonderful way to communicate through the written word. The Care Page was a lifeline of support. We were grateful to have this service provided through CHOC. It was through the Care Page that Ken found it therapeutic to write about Tyler's treatment, his courage, his funny remarks and his inner strength. He was able to keep many friends and family updated about Tyler's battle and in return our family received messages of support, love, and encouragement. To know that so many others from all over the country and even the world were concerned about Tyler was truly like a pillar of strength holding us up through each day of Tyler's treatment.

Tyler received cards almost every day. We had a daily routine, that after the mail came I would open the cards and print out the Care Page messages and give them to Tyler as he sat in his recliner. Not only was I his nurse and mother, but also his secretary. These handwritten personal notes were a testament to the kindness and empathy of the sender and a treasured gift to Tyler.

March brought bitter words. On March 4th, 2004 Tyler and I went to the clinic to discuss the next step in his treatment. Dr. Kirov, who had always been the most positive in Tyler's prognosis and had always stood up for Tyler to receive the most aggressive treatment, matter-of-factly told us the he could no longer offer a cure, only palliative treatment. Tyler was amazingly calm after hearing this news. Once we were home Tyler reached out by phone to tell friends about this heartbreaking news. After talking to several friends, each one offering their words of love and support. Tyler told me, "Well, Pam helped me the most," she said, "Oh, Tyler! You are the lucky one, you get to go to heaven." James M. Barrie, the author of Peter Pan, wrote, *"To die would be an awfully big adventure."* Tyler knew that he would soon be taking that adventure.

For 19 months Tyler and I were bound together like prisoners locked in a cell by this horrible disease and intensive treatment. In an extreme paradox, this horrible situation actually had one small advantage; I always knew where my teenager was and what he was doing. This was a burden to Tyler, to have his mother as a constant companion. But he did not complain, instead he gave me the wonderful gift of his conversation. We enjoyed exploring ideas and insights. He was a combination of preacher, philosopher, and politician.

In the end, these wonderful talks turned to long periods of quiet with short pleadings for rest. My heart broke when Tyler ask, "how much longer?" And when he said, "I'm tired of being sick," I told him, that it was ok for him to no longer fight. I felt more helpless than ever before; all my nursing and mothering skills were now useless. Tyler's once strong body was now a physical prison.

I will treasure these conversations. The ones at the beginning of his treatment, when we talked about new plans for the future after he was "cured," the ones throughout the highs and lows of treatment, and the very short ones for rest at the end. These words both sadden and comfort.

"May the words of my mouth and the meditation of my heart be acceptable in thy sight, O Lord, my strength and my Redeemer." Psalm 19:14

APPLICATION FOR LESSON 3 COMMUNICATION

Key principle: Talk to people about life, dreams, ideas and theories.

Verse to remember: Eph. 4:29

Psalm to read: Psalm 34

Words to study: teach, edify, affirm

Websites to visit: _www.wilber.com_
www.brainyquote.com

Recommended book: Positive Words, Powerful Results
by Hal Urban

Something to do today: Write, call or email a friend, tell them how
they have made a difference in your life.

Spring of 2003 Season of Fighting

By spring we were fighting the cancer full force. Tyler's strong young body was taking a beating. One day he said, "I feel like I'm 17 going on 71." But we had adjusted, as best we could, to our new routine. Our days varied from Tyler being in the hospital fighting a life threatening infection and painful mouth and throat sores to him being home and able to hang out with friends and his Young Marine buddies.

The doctors repeatedly said that they were "happy with his progress." And on May 6th he reached the milestone of completing his 7th round of chemo. We were happy to have reached this milestone, but our hope was tempered by the inclusive results of the CT and PET scans that followed. The cancer was still there, but they could not determine if it was still growing.

On June 6th Tyler endured a five-hour surgery to debulk the remaining cancer and biopsy the tissue. The results were disappointing, the doctors determined that Tyler needed more chemo before he was a candidate for the stem cell transplant.

Tyler's treatment would be extended a few more months. We were discouraged but we would regroup and continue the fight.

Spring 2003 Messages to Tyler

Battles are being fought on all fronts...
Judy DuBose April 10, 2003
Hey Tyler!
Wish I could come up with something really witty that could make you forget about all you are going through, unfortunately I'm not that witty... however, you along with all our other "soldiers" are being prayed for by masses of Christians all over the world - so take heart my friend our God will provide you strength to overcome. You are amazing when it comes to endurance - good thing you had all that training! Just want you to know we love you, and it is about time for you to come over for a special dinner of your choice! Now there is something for you to do, play like you are Emeril and plan the menu for all of us! See you soon!
Love Ken and Judy DuBose

Hey Bud...make those Boots SHINE!
John Dulaney April 27, 2003
Dear Tyler,
I just wanted to let you know that this past weekend the Relay for Life event was held here in Roswell. I am happy to say that over 25 members of the Troop went and walked or ran for three hours. I want you to know that I walked a little over 10 miles on the vita course in your honor. My feet are killing me and my old body aches in places that I didn't know existed, but every time I hurt I realize that it was for a good cause. I am happy to say that HQ had more people participating than any other troop in the entire corps, and I had several say that they were walking in your honor. I was extremely proud of them, as well as I am proud of you for being so

brave. I hope that you are feeling better, and sincerely hope that this next round of chemo is much easier on you.

Dr. DU

NMMI

Always Be Happy!

Gerry Telabangco May 03, 2003

Hi... Tyler, laughter is the best medicine, as the Bible says: "A merry hearth doeth good like a medicine: but a broken a spirit drieth the bones" (Proverbs 17:22, KJV). "Heaviness in the heart of man maketh it stoop: but a good word make it glad" (Proverbs 12:25, KJV).

John wrote to his good friend Gaius: "Beloved, I wish above all things that thou mayest prosper and be in health, even as thy soul prospereth" (3 John 2, KJV).

Trials Increase Appreciation of Life's Joys. When Madam Shumann-Heink was asked to appraise the talents of a young singer, her comment was, "She has a remarkable voice and the promise of a wonderful career, but she will not attain her full power until she has experienced more of the sorrows and heartaches of life." "Sorrow is better than laughter: for by the sadness of the countenance the heart is made better" (Ecc. 7:3, KJV). Adversity enlarges the heart, sharpens the sensibilities, and therefore increases one's capacity to enjoy all the sweet and noble and beautiful experiences of life.

"I have known sorrow - therefore I
May laugh with you, O friend, more merrily
Than those who never sorrowed upon earth
And know not laughter's worth."
Theodosia Garrison

BE HAPPY ALWAYS.

From your brother, Gerry P. Telabangco, Republic of the Philippines

Hey Tyler
Priscilla Swader May 10, 2003

I just keep missing you when I work at CHOC, my once a week deal seems to be the 1 day your not "in" (but it also makes me smile when I don't find you in the hospital!!) Thursday I floated to oncology floor and the nurses know you!! You Charmer!!! I hope to run into you soon.. this web page is great!!

Priscilla Swader

Greeting from LSA Anaconda Iraq
Steve Smith May 11, 2003

Tyler, I saw the back yard BBQ photo. Wish I were there. Glad to hear you are progressing with the treatments. As my mom says, God has got your back! Hot day dusty day here in Iraq. Can't complain...at least it's not cold. We are having a good time and counting the days until we leave. Any good movies out these days? We only get to watch the ones we brought. Well, my time's up.

Take care! Steve

NMMI inspiration
Mark Horton June 17, 2003

Tyler,

When we first moved to Bakersfield in 1996, you would keep my son Kyle updated on all the action movies that we wouldn't let him watch. He has remained very thankful ever since. While following your recovery, Kyle became very interested in NMMI and recently visited the campus in Roswell. Kyle has another year of high school, but has passed the California HS Proficiency Exam. He is ready to ship out to Roswell this fall, but his mother wants him to wait another year.

Thanks for befriending and inspiring my son.

Mark Horton

LESSON 4

HUMOR

"The shortest distance between two people is laughter."
Jerry Lewis

I think what I miss the most about Tyler is his witty sense of humor. He could make me laugh on even the most difficult days. He loved to stay up late and watch the late night comedians, Jay Leno, David Letterman and others. The next day he would repeat the funniest lines from each show. I loved listening to him repeat Leno's one-line jokes or Letterman's top ten.

I don't remember when Tyler first became so astute at humor. It seems like he always had this knack to see the humor in life and to be able to share this humor in a thoughtful and at times irreverent way.

I remember, in August of 2002, before Tyler was diagnosed, we were in Roswell, it was the day of Tyler's matriculation into NMMI. Tyler's Aunt Jana, his grandparents (Granny Annie and Grandpa Walt), Ken and I had taken Tyler to Furr's cafeteria for his "last good meal." I have a precious memory as we enjoyed a lunch together.

With his best Texas drawl, Tyler was telling Jeff Foxworthy's Redneck jokes one after another.

"You might be a redneck if you've unstopped a sink with a shotgun."

"You might be a redneck if you've ever watched a tornado from a lawn chair."

"You might be a redneck if you've ever had a corndog for breakfast."

"You might be a redneck if you have visitation rights to a dog."

He kept us laughing through lunch and afterwards. His memory was sharp and quick.

During Tyler's many hospitalizations, he was blessed to have many visitors and Tyler enjoyed his visitors. What he enjoyed the most about having visitors was making them laugh. So the fourth lesson from Tyler is to see the humor in life, especially in difficult times.

Jennifer L. McMahon writes in The Simpsons and Philosophy, *"Comedy is beneficial because it allows for the examination of serious but often disconcerting subjects in a more comfortable forum."* She goes on to explain that comedy is a useful way to diffuse tension that surrounds difficult subjects. Tyler explained his philosophy like this, "Some people say 'simple minds have simple pleasures,' but I think a complex mind sees the intelligence in pleasure."

Because Tyler's cancer was in his pelvis, he needed to have a colostomy. This of course was a burden for him; but there was no way that he was going to lose this opportunity to use the humor in this situation. Shortly after getting the colostomy, he ask me about the "history of the colostomy." He wanted to know when the first one was done and other facts. His love of learning, communicating and laughter overcame the burden that he was facing. He took pleasure in showing his friends his colostomy, some of them didn't know what one was, but Tyler was happy to teach them. Just a few weeks after his first surgery, we were watching, what else, an episode of the Simpsons; in one scene Homer is skiing down a black diamond slope. Tyler burst into laughter when he reads the name of the slope, "The Colostomizer."

Tyler liked most of his nurses; he liked to observe their personalities and to quickly figure out the best way to interact with them. He enjoyed joking around with them; with his quick wit he could embarrass them without being inappropriate. It became a joke between us that the ostomy nurses were a very unique group. He observed that they really got into the various ostomy supplies. He said, "it's like they are working on a puzzle with all their various bags, patches, glue and paste." But then he kindly said that it was a good thing that someone would do that job.

The Bible says, *"Be joyful in hope, patient in affliction, faithful in prayer"* (Rom.12:12). I don't know if this verse applies to a teenage boy with a colostomy and a sense of humor, but when I read this verse I think of Tyler.

Tyler was a good-looking kid; he had a clean-cut look. He took pride in wearing his uniforms for Young Marines, marching band, and at NMMI. He would spend hours shining his boots and placing his pins just right on his dress uniforms. He even learned how to press a perfect crease in his pants. As a cancer patient, his uniform changed to one of comfort and humor. His uniform now was a T-shirt, loose jeans and black Vans. His favorite T-shirt was one Travis had given him, it was gray and had Homer lying on the couch with his pot belly showing and the words Springfield Unathletic Dept.

On cooler days, he added his "farmer-boy jacket," a well-worn jean jacket that his Uncle Jerry had given him while visiting his farm. The jean jacket originally was worn by Tyler's grandfather, Herschel, 25 years earlier; Tyler never knew his grandfather but he said that wearing the jacket kept him in touch with his West Texas cotton farming roots of four generations.

Tyler never weighed more that 145 lbs. During his treatment, his weight varied between 120 to 110, eating to keep his weight up was a chore. The chemo made him thin and pale. Three weeks after his first round of chemo his hair fell out in a matter of one day. Being a boy, this was no big deal. His visitors frequently complimented him on his "nice looking head." He would rub his smooth scalp and say, "Yeah, girls dig pale, thin, bald guys."

On December 14, 2002, the side effects of the first round of chemo hit Tyler with a vengeance. The nausea, leg pain, and very painful sores down his GI tract consumed his strength but not his sense of humor. As we drove to the hospital, Tyler said, "To quote Ned Flanders, 'I feel like cra-diddly-ap.'"

At times, Tyler used his facial expressions to bring us humor. In April of 2003, Tyler was recovering from one of the very serious infections that the chemo allowed to invade his body. It was a Monday; the doctor came by after checking Tyler's lab results and said that he could go home when his counts begin to go up, "probably by the end of the week." When Tyler gave her "the look," she quickly added, "or sooner." We were amused that he got his message across without saying a word.

During Tyler's treatment, if he wasn't in the hospital, then he would visit the out patient clinic once or twice each week. You all know the routine about doctor appointments and waiting. These clinic visits would involve waiting in the large waiting room, then waiting in the small waiting room a.k.a. the exam room, and finally waiting after the exam for the prescription, tests or whatever else they could think of to make you wait. As Tyler joked, "they wouldn't want to rush you in and out, like they do at the Post Office."

One afternoon we were (yes, you guessed it) waiting in the exam room. We heard a nurse ask, "has anyone seen Tyler's chart?" In a minute, the secretary asks, "has anyone seen Tyler's chart?" Two minutes later another nurse asks, "has anyone seen Tyler's chart?" Tyler and I just looked at each other as we waited, and then broke out into laughter. After the fifth person ask the same question, Tyler opened the door and said, "has anyone seen my chart?"

Tyler shared his sense of humor anytime and anyplace. During a Sunday evening song service, the song leader ask if anyone had a request. Tyler raised his hand and said "703." The teenagers, sitting around Tyler, laughed when the song leader wrote 703 on the white board. The last song in the book was 702.

Tyler's joy brought balance to our difficult circumstances. On June 10, 2003, a few days after his second major abdominal surgery, he described his incision to his grandmother, "It is about 12 inches long, I have 32 staples, and if it went any lower I wouldn't be the man I was when I came in." Bob Hope said, *"I have seen what a laugh can do. It can transform almost unbearable tears into something bearable, even hopeful."*

Even during the last weeks of his life, Tyler maintained his sense of humor. He made jokes about his urostomy bag, his nephrostomy tubes and his pain pump. He teased his Aunt Arlene about her country driving in Orange County. And laughed with his cousins about a Simpsons' episode. He gave Travis a hard time about girls. And he continued to make me laugh. One morning about a month before he died, I was helping him to get dressed; as he looked at all his tubes, bags, IV pump and intrathecal morphine pump he said, "I feel like I could be in a freak show and make a pretty good living, Behold the folly of modern medicine!" he joked.

Paul wrote in Phil. 4:4, *"Rejoice in the Lord always. I will say it again: Rejoice!"* Even though Tyler's body had become a physical prison, he continued to find humor and joy in life. It is a paradox that in this most difficult part of my life Tyler gave me a gift to treasure: a precious memory of him, once again, making me smile.

> *"a time to weep and a time to laugh, a time to mourn and a time to dance," Ecc. 3:4*

APPLICATION LESSON 4 HUMOR

Key principle: See the humor in difficult circumstances. Use laughter daily, it makes learning life's lessons easier.

Verse to remember: Romans 12:12

Psalm to read: Psalm 19

Words to study: joy, rejoice, blessed

Websites to visit: www.snpp.com
www.rd.com

Recommended book: The Simpsons and Philosophy, edited by William Irwin, Mark T. Conrad and Aeon J. Skoble

Something to do today: Be grateful for the gift of humor. Watch an episode of the Simpsons or something that will make you laugh.

Summer 2003 Season to Regroup

As spring turned to summer we would regroup and continue to fight. We would need another plan. Tyler quickly recovered from his second major surgery. While his doctors were investigating the options to give him the best hope for a cure, we used this brief pause in his treatment to make a quick trip to Dallas. We attended Shelly's (Tyler's cousin) wedding. We were grateful for the opportunity to attend the wedding, visit family and friends, and take a break from the storm of DSRCT.

After returning home from Texas, the summer became a roller coaster of treatment plans, emotions, and struggles. Tyler's treatment was now trial and error. A scan at the end of June showed Tyler's cancer was still classified as "active disease." He had another surgery on July 1st; the surgeon was unable to remove all the lesions. But Tyler, as usual, recovered quickly and he celebrated his 18th birthday by going to see the movie The Lord of the Rings and having friends over for a backyard cookout.

He then began a new protocol of chemo, a recipe of three drugs. We needed to hear the words "stable disease," which would give Tyler the go ahead for the stem cell transplant. Tyler endured another surgery in August, from this surgery we were encouraged that the new chemo appeared to be working. He spent the last week of summer in the hospital fighting another infection. Tyler stood firm through the most difficult season so far.

Summer 2003 Messages

Happy 4th!
B. C. Hamilton July 04, 2003

T-man,

I'm hoping that this is a great holiday for you! I'm taking the day to remember those that have sacrificed so much so that we have freedom and may enjoy it. The attitude that I perceive from my veteran friends is that they were willing to do whatever it took to defeat their enemy - no number was too large - no hill too tall - no distance too great. The fight was dirty, and sometimes painful, but although they didn't choose to be there, their attitude was to say, "fine, let's do this". Their actions conveyed a sense of responsibility and maturity beyond their tender years, and provided each of them with a strong sense of honor in knowing that they did the best they could. Each was adamant in saying that their approach to such adversity included taking everything one day at a time, sometimes moment by moment - i.e., just taking the task one step at a time. From reading the updates, I sense the same type of attitude in you. Certainly there is an enemy to face, and a hill to climb, and a distance to cover to reach the "CURE", but I'm certain that YOU and GOD will find the path that fits his will.

GOD bless you! You and your family remain in our daily thoughts and prayers!

As always - love!

b, Lauren and Lindsay

Happy 18th Birthday
Perry Rich July 09, 2003

Tyler,

Hey man whats up i can't believe that you have to do more chemo but i know you can get through this you are the strongest guy i have ever seen but anyway happy birthday i know you aren't going to be able to enjoy it that much but knowing you you'll make the best of it just like everything else i think about and pray for you everyday just keep up the faith leave everything up to god and it will be ok but anyway i will talk to you later man

Perry Rich

Cadet NMMI

Thinking of You and Caring About You
Bud and Berniece Baker July 11th 2003

Hi Tyler,

Just read your care page. It said tomorrow is a hospital day, but it seems like the doctors have it all planned and are now ready to get down to getting you to the finish line……. that is what we all are looking forward to; but also in times such as these we learn patience and I know you have done a great job with that.

Love,

Bud and Berniece

Glad to hear the good news
Pete Kinser August 18, 2003

Tyler, we are so glad that things went well and that you are doing so well. We are proud of your strength and endurance, and of course, I personally like the fact that you are BALDER than me. Maybe soon you will become a "well rounded citizen" like your friend, the writer.

Go with God!!

Pete

Courageous Tyler
Ardus Ward August 30, 2003

Tyler, Judy and Ken, So happy you are doing so great, Tyler. Seems prayer does help.

Hope you get to get out more and see more movies, and go out with your friends.

Love to all of you.

Mary Etta & Ardus

Hello from Tampa!!!
Newton Walker September 08, 2003
Hello Tyler!

I am so pleased with your progress! May the Lord continue to bring you improvement. From what I read, you are a great kid. Your courage and might in your fight to conquer this illness is admirable. No wonder your caregivers like you so much!

Give your family an extra hug tonight as you are so blessed to have them. Not just any family could get you through these times. It takes a special and godly family and clearly that you have.

We continue to pray that much better days are soon to come for you and your family. May the Lord bless you and your family and always keep you all within the protection of His love. May the Lord give you strength to overcome the occasional bumps in the road ahead and firm assurance that you will win a grand victory over this illness!

Brotherly in Christ,
Newton Walker

Hey man!
Keith Houchin September 14, 2003
Hey man, glad to hear your keeping those nurses on their toes. Stay

out of trouble and hope you get out of the hospital soon. Talk to ya later!
Keith

Hey Tyler!
Emily Robbins September 17, 2003
Hey Tyler! I am really glad that everything is starting to look better again! I know it is taking a while, but I have total faith that you will be the same old you after the transplant and after this whole process. Just remember your friends in Bakersfield and everywhere else keep you in their minds and pray for you! Well, I wish you a lot of love and luck!
Your sister in Christ,
Emily A. Robbins

LESSON 5

COMPASSION

"What do we live for, if it is not to make life less difficult for each other." George Eliot

Tyler had a talent and desire to help others, especially those that were younger than him or less mature than him in some way. The help that Tyler offered was given through his compassion for others. Webster's defines compassion as *a feeling of deep sympathy or sorrow for someone, accompanied by a desire to alleviate the suffering.* Or in my "keep it simple" style of thinking; compassion is simply, "desire to help."

Compassion like love, to be helpful needs to be transferred from a feeling to acts and deeds. Sometimes the only action needed is to simply be there, to sit and talk or sit and listen. Sometimes we help with a physical act or job, something as simple as giving someone a ride or more involved as helping them move to a new dorm or apartment. The Bible says. *"Be kind and compassionate to one another"* (Eph.4:32). Sometimes we need to help others by helping them to grow or gain knowledge. The Bible says, *"We urge you, brothers, warn those who are idle, encourage the timid, help the weak, be patient with everyone"* (I Thess. 5:14). So the fifth lesson from Tyler is to find ways to help others. Be compassionate.

Tyler's heart was full of compassion. He demonstrated this compassion by helping others in two ways. He would help in a time of need by giving comfort, doing something for another person, or mentoring them. The other way he helped was to teach them what they needed to do to help themselves. This second way of helping usually requires more time and energy, Tyler found the best way to accomplish this was to lead through service

Let me summarize this thought with a simple diagram:

                               Comfort to others (help others) mentor

Compassion   or

(desire to help)   Lead through service (help others help them-selves) teach

In most of our relationships there is a balance between these two kinds of compassion. Tyler had a talent for finding this balance. He found this balance by getting to know your personality traits. He would engage you in one of his delightful conversations. He didn't care for idle talk about the weather or gossip; he would ask you about your thoughts on different topics. Then once he got to know you, you could count on him as a friend, mentor, and teacher.

Lead through service, this was Tyler's MO (mode of operation) in helping others help themselves. I think that his talent as a drill instructor in the Young Marines is the best example of this. Tyler loved being a drill instructor. He loved to teach and mentor a new recruit class. Tyler's goal as a drill instructor was "to make sure that every Young Marine was getting something out of the program." He had a talent to give each recruit just the right kind of instruction and motivation they needed. Sometimes the motivation was a direct order, sometimes a pat on the back; and at times Tyler knew he needed to use discipline as motivation. In the Young Marines discipline usually means, "OK knucklehead, give me twenty push-ups!" But Tyler knew that discipline is best given with compassion. He strove to acquire the 14 character traits of a Young Marine NCO. These are:

Integrity	Justice
Knowledge	Enthusiasm
Courage	Bearing
Decisiveness	Endurance
Dependability	Unselfishness
Initiative	Loyalty
Tact	Judgement

Tyler added compassionate to this list.

Tyler's thought process was analytical and mathematical; he would look at things practically and had a lot of common sense. He knew that showing compassion wasn't just the right thing to do, but the practical thing to do. Your words and actions of today will have consequences in days to come. Compassion today will build benefits tomorrow. It is one of the best investments you can make. C. S. Lewis said, *"Good and evil both increase at compound interest. That is why the little decisions you and I make every day are of such infinite importance. The smallest good act today is the capture of a strategic point from which, a few months later, you may be able to go on to victories you never dreamed of. An apparently trivial indulgence in lust or anger today is the loss of a ridge or railway line or bridge head from which the enemy may launch as attack other wise impossible."*

Because Tyler was 17 when he was diagnosed, he received his treatment through pediatric oncologists and a children's hospital. This gave Tyler a somewhat unique experience. There were of course other teens at the hospital but for the most part Tyler was much older than most of the other pediatric patients. Tyler's tender heart was full of compassion for these younger patients. As Tyler spent so much time at the hospital we often heard the cries of other patients in the next room. Each time Tyler would say, "I feel sorry for that child," his heart was touched.

Comforting others goes both ways and Tyler received a full measure of comfort from others. Throughout Tyler's 19 months of treatment we had to be prepared to be admitted to the hospital at a moment's notice. We quickly learned to keep the things needed for an admission in the back of our Jeep, among these things were the blanket that his Aunt Arlene had made for him, books, his own pillow, phone book and calling card, and the universal TV remote. Included in these items was Tyler's rainbow afghan. Because of its' bright colors, almost everyone that came into Tyler's room ask about the rainbow afghan. I had started the afghan when we were living in Arlington, Texas and Tyler was 4 years old. I was a beginner at crocheting and was slowly working on the afghan. Granny Annie, as all the grandkids call my mother, came to visit. I ask her to help me with the afghan and in a matter of a day it was finished. Tyler found comfort in both the rainbow afghan and Arlene's blanket; they were symbols of love and compassion.

Tyler also had contact with younger patients through his frequent clinic visits. There he became friends with a precious 8-year-old girl named Rachel. Rachel was a ray of sunshine. She became a comfort to Tyler and could make him smile. It became a contest between Tyler and Rachel to see who would get finished with their clinic visit first. The 'winner' got to tell the other one,

"I'm outa here!"

Tyler last visit to the clinic was two weeks before he died. That day Rachel's mom made a picture of Tyler and Rachel. After Tyler died they sent us the picture along with a drawing of Rachel's. Both the drawing and the picture are precious treasures and a beautiful illustration of compassion. Thank you sweet Rachel.

I conclude this lesson with a request to help others that continue to fight cancer and other illnesses. Tyler's treatment included over 100 transfusions of packed red blood cells and /or platelets. The chemo drugs ravished his bone marrow, the source for new blood cells. The Bible tells us that life is in the blood, both physically and spiritually. Leviticus 17:11 says, *" For the life of a creature is in the blood, and I have given it to you to make atonement for yourselves on the altar; it is the blood that makes atonement for one's life."* The word blood is used over 400 times in the Bible. Christ gave his blood for us to be healed spiritually (I Peter 1:18-19). Our physical bodies need a healthy daily supply of blood cells. God's word is perfect and beautiful; He gives us a physical picture to teach us a spiritual truth. Life is in the blood; each transfusion gave Tyler the much-needed life for his thin body.

Each pint of the critical transfusion was the gift of a compassionate donor. Each pint of blood donated can be used to save three lives. Units are separated into their three components. Red cells are used to treat patients with anemia, plasma is used to treat surgical and burn patients, and platelets are used to treat leukemia and bone marrow transplant patients. 16,000,000 pints of blood are donated annually, but there is still a shortage of more than 250,000 each year. Donating is easy and can be done every 60 days; this is truly a priceless gift and a gesture of remarkable compassion. Please consider becoming a blood donor. A web site for information about donation is www.bloodsaves.com.

"If your actions create a legacy that inspires others to dream more, learn more, do more and become more, then, you are an excellent leader." Dolly Parton

APPLICATION LESSON 5 COMPASSION

Key principle: Be compassionate toward others, lead through service.
Be a mentor. Be a teacher.

Verse to remember: Col. 3:12

Psalm to read: Psalm 121

Words to study: compassion, comfort

Websites to visit: www.bloodsaves.com
www.volunteermatch.org

Recommended book: Abounding Grace by M. Scott Peck, M.D.

Something to do today: Research groups, organizations, or clubs and consider becoming a volunteer.

Fall 2003 Season of Hope

The first day of fall brought renewed hope. On the first afternoon of this new season, Tyler was discharged from the hospital. He had fought off another serious infection. He walked out of the hospital to a sunny, warm day and said, "freedom!" We prayed that this new season would bring Tyler health and strength.

The new chemo protocol slowed the growth of the cancer, but it also lowered his blood counts for so long that each round of chemo was delayed 2-3 weeks. Tyler used the extra time to see movies, go to the shooting range, go to church, and, of course, have discussions. One discussion centered around the statement by our friend, Chris. He said, "God is not a God of self-help, but a God of salvation." Tyler also talked about things he was grateful for; drugs for pain and nausea, being home, mangos, and iced tea.

On November 1st Tyler had been engaged in this storm for one year. He had finished the "regular" chemo and remained hopeful. On November 10th we rejoiced at the "all clear" for the transplant. We allowed ourselves to dream that Tyler would be cured.

But there were more obstacles to come; Tyler spent Thanksgiving in the hospital with a severe case of shingles. Nothing about this was easy. On December 10th Tyler began the much anticipated stem cell transplant. I prayed Psalm 121:8 *"the Lord will watch over your coming and going both now and forever."*

As fall turned into winter, we took each day as best we could. Tyler remained in the ICU for the holidays. We would celebrate when he was discharged. I prayed that winter would be the season of healing.

Fall 2003 Messages to Tyler

Be Tough!
Jackie Anderson September 30, 2003

Hi Tyler,

You don't know me but it sure seems like I know you - I work with your dad - and if your anything like him, your a special person (obviously). I just want you to know that you are constantly in my thoughts and prayers and I have been really praying for you - forget the wimpy prayers, only heavy duty ones! Be tough! Get your counts up and get these treatments behind us! Hope your feeling better soon... God bless you.

Jackie Anderson

Thinking of you always Rat Buddy
Maggie Adams October 01, 2003

hey teague its good to hear that you have been okay. things here at nmmi have been very busy. its different coming back being a private. i enjoy it but i miss the days of being a RAT. well i was thinking of you and am praying for you. we miss you much.

sincerely, maggie adams

Hey Tyler
Jill Lopez November 06, 2003

Just letting you know we are praying extra hard for a good report tomorrow and Monday. You are to be admired because a true character of a person can be judged by his reaction to the things that we cannot control. Your attitude and humor (along with the prayers) have got you through the year and will continue in your progress.

Love, Jill

Time to lift JESUS higher.

Felix Walker November 11, 2003

Hi Tyler

Good news is always good; Jesus was the first good news. HE DIED ON THE CROSS SO THAT WE CAN LIVE. BY HIS STRIPES WE ARE HEALED, so to GOD be the glory great things he has done. You are healed.

Felix

What WONDERFUL News

Joan McCallister November 11, 2003

Hi Tyler, Judy and Ken,

This is the greatest news.....just what everyone has been praying for....Tyler, what a year you have had.....but your faith never seemed to waiver.........you are such a witness to all.....and of course so are you Mom and Dad.... I know you still have some hard times ahead.....but you can see that beautiful light at the end of this long, long, tunnel.....Thanks to God for HIS unconditional love and HIS care for us....."WHAT A MIGHTY GOD WE SERVE" !!!!!

We love you, Joan and Tommy

Keep Pluggin'

Randy Hilburn November 26, 2003

Wow, Just what you need now is the shingles! Keep doing what you've got to do, Tyler. Under the circumstances, I know that's got to be hard. One of our jobs is to keep praying along with yours and the prayers of your family and friends. God be with you all.

Love, Randy Hilburn

As they say, this too will pass.

Lorraine Lane November 26, 2003

No matter what, there is still much to be thankful for. I am thankful to know someone like you. Our best holiday wishes and prayers to you and your family.

The Lanes

Keepin you in my prayers

Lisa Canup December 11, 2003

Hey Tyler! I'm comin home tomorrow, and I can't wait till I get to see you again. Good luck with everything. Remember that if you ever need to talk or anything at all, you can call me. I'm always here for you and your family. God is with you, and that is the most comforting thing that you should know. I will see you soon. You are continually in my thoughts and prayers. ROMANS 8:28

Love,

Lisa

Just keep taking it one day at a time.

Cathy Kinser December 11, 2003

Dear Tyler,

Anton Chekhov said, "Any idiot can face a crisis....... It's this day-to-day living that wears you out." You handle both the crisis and the day-to-day with such grace and courage.

I love you,

Cathy

Hi Again From Canada's East Coast

John Woods December 17, 2003

Hi Tyler.

My name is John Woods (Halifax, Nova Scotia) and I wrote to you several months ago. I want you to know that just because you have not heard from me, it doesn't mean I'm not here. I check in on your condition regularly. More importantly, I pray for you every morning. You are at the top of my list, ahead of my own family members.

As each day passes, I find that your health is becoming more important to me and I am ever grateful that you are receiving the very best in medical care and support from your great family. I also take consolation in the knowledge that I'm just one of the many who pray daily for your recovery.

I have a 32 year-old son who is a hematologist and who is presently working in the bone marrow field at Sonnybrook Hospital in Toronto, Ontario. He does not come home often and I miss him. But knowing that he is sharing his gifts in the healing of others provides me with much comfort. I know your doctors love you like their own son, making your family all the bigger. If it were possible, I would like nothing better that to accompany my son to meet you and your family. You are a great, great young man and I know God is with you. As we enter into the final days leading up to Christmas, I will make sure you are ever present in my prayers. God blesses you Tyler.

Best Wishes from Halifax
Dwight Jeans December 22, 2003
Tyler, Ken and Mrs. Teague: "Merry Christmas" to you all and may the New Year bring much joy to your family.

Tyler, your journey is one of courage and faith and I and others, I am sure, would like to thank you for this gift to us.

I will continue to say a prayer for you and wish you all the Best Christmas has to offer. Dwight Jeans, Halifax, Canada

To the Teague Family
Melody Biddle December 24, 2003
I have been reading your updates with great interest and much anticipation of good news. Today as I awoke to a fresh blanket of snow on our lawn here in Indiana, I am happy to read that good news has landed in CA!

Tyler, you are truly a fighter, and I cannot imagine how proud your parents must be of you, how precious you must be to them. And life must have such magic for you....you are tired of being prodded, poked, cut on, stitched up, but here you are, making your own blood! Who says young people are all slackers?

As you open your eyes on Christmas morning, I hope that you will know that many many people are praying for you, and petitioning our Lord and Savior on your behalf. Just think of all the thoughts, prayers and cards and visits you have received in the time that you have been beating the daylights out of this cancer!!

I am so excited for you, and hope that the coming days will bring you even more good news, strength, and wonderful memories with those you love and hold dear.

Merry Christmas Teague family. I know that the first of many wonderful presents have arrived for you.

Give praise to our God and our Lord and Savior Jesus Christ.

Hugs
Melody Biddle
Indianapolis, Indiana

LESSON 6

PATIENCE

"Our conversations reflect our values; our actions mirror our maturity; our habits reveal our character." Bill Ward

As Ken and I raised Travis and Tyler we quickly became aware that one of the most valuable lessons that a parent can teach a child is *delayed gratification*. Travis and Tyler grew up in the 80's and 90's, two decades that saw tremendous growth in technology, materialism and affluence. It seemed like every week there was a newer and better toy, video game, computer or any other number of things to enthrall kids. So a lesson in delayed gratification was not just a good idea but a necessary one. We were fortunate that while Travis and Tyler enjoyed these new gadgets, most of the time they were willing to wait for Christmas, their birthday or save up their allowance. As most parents know, often the desire for the new toy quickly fades as another one appears.

This valuable lesson of delayed gratification if learned in childhood can be the basis for being a responsible adult. Tom Morris Ph.D., the head of the Morris Institute for Human Values said,

"There are two different forms of dissatisfaction in human life. There is first the dissatisfaction of acquisition. This is when you're not satisfied with what you have. You want more stuff." He continues, *"The second form of dissatisfaction is the dissatisfaction of aspiration. This is when you are not satisfied with what you are and want to become something better. You want to be wiser, to know more, to experience more, to develop more talents, to be a better person."*

He then explains that the dissatisfaction of acquisition feeds on itself, the more you give in to it and try to satisfy it, the more it grows. The dissatisfaction of aspiration is very different. You aspire to be better or accomplish more. You are not satisfied where you are existentially, you want to do and be more. This dissatisfaction of aspiration can be a healthy goad for growth.

You can only use so many material goods at a time, one car, one pair of shoes, one I-pod; but you will never be wise enough, joyful enough, spiritual enough. Learn when enough is enough and when it isn't.

To practice delayed gratification will help you build self-discipline. Self-discipline is the foundation of many valuable habits, i.e. budgeting time and money, moderation in eating and exercising, being on time, prioritizing how time is spent, seeking knowledge and wisdom, planning and purposing for each day.

These habits can be the foundation for personal responsibility. My definition of personal responsibility is to be a good steward of the blessings, privileges and talents that you have received. The habit of personal responsibility will open the doors of fulfillment and contentment and close the doors of materialism and selfishness.

In summary:

Delayed gratification $\rightarrow$ Self discipline $\rightarrow$ Personal responsibility

I have said all this to build a case for the importance of delayed gratification. Included in delayed gratification are patience and waiting. And that introduces Tyler's sixth lesson; practice patience rather than self pity. The Bible teaches us about patience and waiting.

First, we must recognize that *God is in control.* In the book of Job three chapters, 38-40, beautifully illustrate this fact. Job's friends had offered their words of wisdom and advice and their words were many. But eventually after 37 chapters of discourses from his friends, God speaks and asks Job some questions. Job does not have any answers. After hearing God speak he was humbled and said, "I know that you can do all things." He knew that God was in control. These three chapters of Job 38-40 are beautiful. Please take time to read them. Then read Psalm 46. The 10th verse says, *"Be still and know that I am God;"* what a comforting verse to a young man facing a terrible disease.

Tyler once said, "I feel like Job." And although Tyler had all the advantages of modern medicine and pain medication, I think that he also acted like Job. Tyler was patient through his suffering. Soldier Boy continued steadfast and courageously.

Tyler carried the burden of illness as well as anyone could. He could tolerate the burden of nausea, pain, and chemo. He rarely complained. The one burden that he tolerated the least was "being special." Yes, being special is a burden. Tyler knew that his circumstances might be unusual. He felt many emotions, but special was not one of them. He knew that he was a unique creation by God, just like we all are, but he felt like he was just an ordinary teenage boy. Just an average teenage boy dealing with an illness the best way he could. Tyler missed being ordinary; he quickly grew tired of all the attention that this illness brought. He longed to just be ordinary; he just wanted to go to school, hang out with friends, and get his first job.

"It is better to light a candle than curse the darkness." This

Chinese proverb is the motto for the Candlelighters Childhood Cancer Foundation. Waiting on God and practicing patience doesn't mean doing nothing and procrastinating. When difficult days come, it is ok to be sad, but don't have a pity party. Well, maybe a short one, but then get up and metaphorically light a candle. Remember, be engaged in life.

Throughout his treatment, Tyler remained engaged in life. On his 18th birthday, July 9th 2003, he made sure that he registered to vote; and later that year he proudly voted in the governor's race in California. He maintained contact with his 'RAT' buddies at NMMI, keeping up with their activities and even going to visit them once. He continued to work with the Young Marines and observe their drills. He listened to the news and followed the presidential campaign. He played chess with his friends, especially Keith. He continued to flirt with the girls. And whenever he was able, he attended worship services and Bible class. On February 29th, 2004 he eloquently spoke before the church about love and a new perspective. In his sermon, he made the point that it is better to DO the smallest deed than to talk about great intentions. Yes, we need to be patient and delay or forgo the accumulation of material things, but being patient doesn't mean sitting and doing nothing. When we are faced with darkness and difficulties don't wait till tomorrow to light a candle. Because God is in control and He will give you strength.

"Be still and know that I am God." Psalm 46:10

APPLICATION LESSON 6 PATIENCE

Key principle: Practice patience rather than self pity.
Learn to delay gratification.

Verse to remember: Psalm 27:14

Psalm to read: Psalm 46

Words to study: patience, wait

Websites to visit: www.cccf.org
www.forbetterlife.org

Recommended book: Philosophy for Dummies
by Tom Morris, Ph.D.

Something to do today: Read Job 38-40

Winter 2004 Season of Searching

As the short days of winter gradually lengthened Tyler slowly recovered from the stem cell transplant. We tried to remain optimistic. Some of the doctors' comments were not encouraging, but we continued to faithfully pray for a complete cure. Tyler was discharged from the hospital on January 6th. He said we just wanted to go home sit in his recliner and drink iced tea. The small measure of hope that the transplant gave us soon faded. The cancer continued to grow. On January 22nd, Tyler faced another surgery to remove a turnip size tumor.

We searched for answers, help, and miracles. Tyler was given two more chemo drugs, but any treatment was like pouring a cup of water on a raging fire. Tyler remained Tyler; he talked about his new perspective on life. He said, he used to be religious but now he was spiritual.

February and March gave us a paradox. The visits with the doctors brought fear and discouragement; but the end of the aggressive treatment gave us faith and perseverance. During February and March, all of Tyler's treatment was done as an outpatient. This gave us precious time to spend with family and friends.

Tyler made the most of this precious time. He went to a shipping out party for one of his Marine buddies; he went to a youth forum at one of the local churches; he made one more trip to Bakersfield. He went to visit friends and teachers at his high school and, of course, went to a few movies including, The Passion of the Christ.

During the day, I continued my duties as mother, nurse, and secretary. During the night I searched for courage and hope. I again turned to Psalm 121, I prayed, *"He will not let your foot slip, he who watches over you will not slumber."*

Winter 2004 Messages to Tyler

So glad you are home.
Ann Shields January 06, 2004
Dear Tyler,
So glad you have escaped from the hospital and was able to walk out. Hope you get to stay home for a long time and celebrate the holidays out of the hospital and open your Christmas presents. Sorry Travis and your friends had to go back to school, but maybe some of those cute girls are still hanging around for you to go to the movies with.
Love you, Granny Annie

SO GLAD TYLER IS HOME !!!!
Joan McCallister January 06, 2004
Hi Tyler, Judy and Ken..........We are so thankful that Tyler is once again home........."walked out of the hospital" and back to the comfort of his home.....iced tea and all!!!! I just talked with Granny Annie....of course she was so happy....We will continue to pray for that complete recovery.....no wimpy prayers 'ever' as Ken as instructed. Know that we love you, Joan

Hi Tyler:
Polly Hamilton January 07, 2004
I am really happy you got to go home. There is no place like home, I like to stay home and sit in my recliner and drink tea. We must be kinfolk.
God Bless you and I love you, Polly

Hello...
Kerry Robbins January 16, 2004
Tyler,
I am so proud of you right now. It is so encouraging to see your commitment to Christ and your concerns with His Word. I am so glad that you're doing well, despite your delay and all. I pray that the surgery that is scheduled works out as well...Tyler, hearing about your ongoing faith throughout this whole ordeal has really made me examine my own faith and lean on Him even more...it is amazing how when you seem to need it the most, one can come across passages throughout Bible pertaining to the exact situation that you yourself are dealing with at that time...when I was baptized your mom sent me a letter, along with a card with Phillipians 4:13 on it ((which is hanging on my mirror))...always remember that verse, because it is so true...and Joshua 1:9...
Hope you're up to coming for a visit to good ole Bakersfied some time soon...we all miss you, and hope you feel better!
In Christian Love,
Kerry

Thanks for the news
Jane Hensley January 22, 2004
Glad to hear that the surgery is over and that Tyler is already giving the nurses a hard time. I hope he continues to improve and will be able to eat soon. Take care. Jane

To Tyler
Jana Brooke February 03, 2004
Hello, Tyler
Hope that you are feeling well today and those platelets gave you a boost. We think of you every day and ask God to bless you and your mom and dad. I have the picture of you that your mom sent on my

refrigerator. You are sitting out in the sun smiling. Seeing your smiling face reminds how special you are. I hope that you will be able to come visit us soon.

Love

Aunt Jana

Thanks for the Fun

Dawn Green February 25, 2004

Hey Tyler,

I just wanted to say thanks for hanging out with me on Saturday. I really had a great time getting lunch and just catching up. I enjoyed the many different topics of our conversations. I hope that you are continuing to feel well and that you're having fun eating. We need to hang out again soon. I hope that your meeting with your oncologist goes well on Thursday. I'll be praying for that as well as your blood counts. Have an awesome week and I'll talk to you soon.

Love In Christ,

Dawn Green

So Tyler......

Melody Biddle February 28, 2004

I understand that you are rock climbing, and right now you are between a rock and a hard place. What to do?

There is no right or wrong answer here. You have no way of knowing what the outcome will be, whichever option you choose.

This is a time for prayer, and let me just tell you that I am praying very hard for you Tyler, and your family, and the doctors and nurses. I know that you all have your hearts full, and so I am petitioning God to give you all ease, that He will send His angels to comfort you all.

Tyler, I am so thankful that you have accepted Jesus as your Lord and Savior. It gives me such relief to know that you have prioritized Him in your life, and that you have His desires at heart.

I know that you want the medical stuff to stop. I know that you are tired of hospitals, needles, tests, scans, doctor offices, emergency rooms, transplants, transfusions, medication, being tired, being bald (maybe, but I have to admit you look cute), a limited social life, and all these restrictions on your life.

I am sad that you have had to spend, what, eighteen months of your life with your dreams on hold, trying to give the cancer clear indication that you do not want it in your life. What an annoying distraction!!!

I am happy though that you have used this time for good—you have looked at your relationship with God, and made corrections that you felt were needed. You are taking care of the temple of God that was given to you, and are doing your best to weed out the physical evils as well as the spiritual evils.

I just want you to know that, while I do not know what you are going through, I am thinking about you, and keeping you in my thoughts each and everyday.

God is with you, Tyler. He doesn't like to see you going through these things either. But, as with Job, He is with you, and you belong to HIM, and while He cannot give you any answer as to why this has happened to you, HE will always be with you.

Prayers and friendship,
Melody
Oaklandon, Indiana

Tyler's sermon on February 29, 2004

A friend has asked me what do I think when somebody gets up and gives a prayer in front of the congregation for me? My answer was that when it occurs it's a nice thought and its encouraging — not so much for myself, but to know that there are so many other faithful Christians in the world. I believe that prayer can give healing strength in ways that we cannot even comprehend. What really matters to me is that when I'm in a hospital bed for weeks on-end and feel like giving up, it gives me the strength to carry on. Although, I don't think voicing a prayer out loud in-front of the congregation is necessary for prayer to give the healing strength; it can give a powerful message that, can sometimes be heard in ways that may move us. Although, I don't think my words here tonight will be anything that hasn't been said before, I hope that in some-way they might mean something to somebody.

I would like to thank all of my fellow brothers and sisters in Christ for all of the support they have given me. Whether it is calls, cards, conversations, visits, prayers, food, or any other type of support, it really helps me and my family get through this hard and difficult time. Besides the physical support it gives me and my family, this support and faith of Christians has allowed me to grow in my spirituality throughout the past year and a half. I recognize that my situation is unique with an ability to show me a new perspective that might not often be seen, but by no means do I consider it tougher than some of the situations that many of you might be going through.

My lesson here is on the basics of Christianity and how a new perspective can sometimes reestablish you in a stronger way and allow you to grow in your Christianity. Let me assure you that you are a tool of God and you will be used to serve the good purpose. You may be used through good and show that righteousness is rewarded in the end, or you may serve God through evil and show that evil is punished. That is your choice, but it will serve the greater good.

A new perspective is a term that is used a lot. In my case, not only do I have to realize a new perspective but also I am thrown in to one so rapidly that I can remember what it was like before I was diagnosed. I can remember what mattered to me then and look at what matters to me now that I am diagnosed with cancer and have had to go through this process. When one looks at what was important to them before and looks at what is important to them now there will be differences but where those overlap it shows what is of true importance. To put it simply, God is what is of true importance and our Christianity.

The entire basis of our Christianity is faith. If you don't have that faith, then in that situation there are some things that you can do to help you grow. The first question anybody has to ask themselves is if they believe in a God at all, a higher power. And there are some people in the world who believe that there is no God. Without a higher purpose, without something above us then life has no meaning and there is no reason not to do what you feel like. Once you chose to believe in a higher power you can then look at the religions of the world to find out about this God. Surely if there is a higher power he has given us a message. Since I have been diagnosed, I have had a lot of time to study some areas that I have found interesting and one of those areas is the other religions. I can tell you right now that none of them make any sense when compared against Christianity.

After one realizes that Christ is the one who is true and decides to follow Christ, one must follow the basic teachings of the New Testament. These basic teachings are quite simple. They require you to be a good person. Even people of the world tend to follow these requirements to an extent. These teachings require you to be a good person — to treat other people, as you would like to be treated. Even non-believing people of the world do this because they recognize they benefit from following these principals. They may not do it because they believe in a higher power but do it because they do not want to be treated badly. However, if you follow these teachings because of a faith in God, it can lead you to see how the Bible and the rest of the teachings fit into place and you can see the higher power of God in work through other human beings and in nature itself.

The law that God commands us to do, that is the most important, is to love. To love the Lord your God with all of your heart and all your soul and all your mind and then this is followed with the second law of to love your fellow neighbor. Many people are confused as to what love is. Some people think love is an emotional feeling that one gets related to the opposite sex. Although sexuality does have a purpose in this life, that is not true love. True love is an intellectual decision to sacrifice for other people for the better good. Love can sometimes be a symbiotic relationship in which both people attain something greater out of it. But sometimes it requires sacrifice on your behalf or on somebody else's behalf. Sometimes it requires you to rebuke somebody for doing wrong. But to do so with a kind heart and not for your own good but for theirs.

With my new perspective on life, I can see how love has been shown in my life. And I can see that God ultimately is in control and whether or not we can see how our actions can play out to the greater good we know that they will.

Two years ago, I had my life all planned out. I was going to go to New Mexico Military Institute for a year and then transfer to the Navel Academy become a Marine Corp Officer to serve my country. Now that has all changed. At first I thought why me? I was a good person. I know now that it has allowed me to grow spiritually and faithfully in ways I would never have been able to attain otherwise. In Romans 8:28 we read, *"And now we know that God causes all things to work together for good to those who are called according to his purpose."*

Two years ago, I thought I was knowledgeable and I thought that I had wisdom. I was making good grades I graduated a year early from high school — started college. Now I recognized some things hold true as seen in Ecclesiastes 1:8 *"For with much wisdom comes much sorrow."* The more knowledge the more grief. The problem with knowledge is that it causes grief. Although it allows us to see some greater truths and build us in our faith, we read in I Corinthians 8:1 *" Knowledge puffs up but love builds up."*

Two years ago, I was physically strong, fit, healthy. Then I got cancer and now I can barely walk a short distance without being tired. But you can read in Isaiah 40:30-31 *"Though youth grow weary and tired, and vigorous young men stumble badly, yet those who wait for the Lord will gain new strength. They will mount up wings like eagles. They will run and not grow tired. They will walk and not become weary."* I now know that spiritual endurance is of greater importance than any physical endurance.

This might be the biggest one. Two years ago, I thought I was so independent. I didn't need anybody to help me with anything, and I could do everything for myself. Then I was diagnosed, and now sometimes I need help just getting out of bed. But you can read in Galatians 6:2 *"Carry each other's burdens and in this way you will full fill the law of Christ."* Now I know that I need others, not only to help me physically, but also to encourage me in my faith and spiritually.

Two years ago, I was proud of my accomplishments and I put my trust and my faith in my abilities. Then I was diagnosed and found that my past challenges were very small compared to what I was now facing. You can read in Proverbs 3:5-6 *"Trust in the Lord with all of year heart and lean not on your own understanding. In all of your ways acknowledge him and he will make your path straight."* I now know that one must fully trust in the Lord.

I now go back to the subject of love. The basis of all of our actions should be love. It should be an intellectual decision on our part to chose for the greater good. In the words of Mother Teresa "The smallest deed done is better than the grandest intentions." Things have occurred in my life that other people would pass off and shrug as a small thing, but they have had a large affect on me. When I was first diagnosed a lot of my worldly friends were interested in my situation and they would call and ask how was I doing and they would ask what was expected later on. After about two weeks many of those calls died off, but my Christian brothers and sisters are the ones that continued on. It was beyond their own curiosity, but an actual concern about my health. What is important in life is the effect that you have on other people and I can assure you this has had an effect on me. The love that you show and the love seen by your example will be greater than any accomplishment that you could ever achieve. In 2 Corinthians 5:7 we read, *"We live by faith and not by sight."* I now know that we live on God's promises and not God's explanations.

We read in Isaiah 53:5 *"He was pierced for our transgressions, he was crushed for our inequities the punishment that brought us peace was upon him, and by his wounds we are healed."* Although I continue to struggle in my physical battle, I know and I trust in the Lord and can have faith that he will heal me and anyone who will ask him to, spiritually and that we will live forever in heaven.

I would like to finish by thanking everyone once again for their support. If you want to know why life is the way that life is, and want to believe in something greater but don't know what it is, you will find it in the Word of God.

LESSON 7

PERSEVERANCE

"The road to the promise land runs past Sinai." C. S. Lewis

Tyler's favorite book in the Bible was Ecclesiastes. He liked this book because in it Solomon discusses the puzzles of life, the questions of life, the what if questions, the why questions. This intrigued Tyler. He saw the book of Ecclesiastes as a book of Theology and King Solomon the professor. King Solomon wrote in Ecc. 3:10, *"I have seen the burden (travail) that God has laid on men."* To paraphrase, 'life is difficult!' So we ask why? Why does God allow men burdens, trials, storms, tests or suffering?

First, we must distinguish between burdens we bring on ourselves through dishonesty, stupidity, and pride and those that life brings us. Those we bring on ourselves bring the consequences also; we "reap what we sow." For these burdens we must pray for wisdom to not be stupid. In the movie Thirteen Conversations about One Thing, one of the characters paraphrases the philosopher S. Keirkegaard, "life only makes sense looking back, too bad we have to live it forward." We must live our lives looking forward, think about the decisions that you make today with the future in mind. Ask yourself how will this decision or action affect tomorrow or next week or years later. So while we all make mistakes and foolish decisions, again, pray for wisdom to not be stupid. By limiting the problems we bring on ourselves we save those precious problem-solving, life-coping skills for the problems that life bring us.

Life is difficult; we are spiritual beings on a physical journey. Victor Frankl, the author and psychiatrist who spent three years in Nazi concentration camps, wrote in Man's Search for Meaning, *"What was really needed was a fundamental change in our attitude toward life. We had to learn ourselves and furthermore teach the despairing men, that it really did not matter what we expect from life, but rather what life expected from us. We need to stop asking about the meaning of life, and instead to think of ourselves as those being questioned by life, daily and hourly. Our answer must consist, not in talk and meditation, but in right action and in right conduct. Life ultimately means taking the responsibility to find the right answer to its problem and to fulfill the tasks which it constantly sets for each individual."*

Since every person is a unique individual, each of these problems are unique and the response is unique. Tyler and I discussed these unlimited interactions between individuals and problems. We talked about how some people face major trials with fortitude and others need help with much smaller trials. Tyler said that it was not our place to distinguish who had a harder trial or their response to it. Our duty was to help and encourage based on opportunity, not judgement. Even after months of treatment, we were confused and perplexed that Tyler had the burden of cancer. This is one of those discussions we had while we were waiting in the clinic.

Dr. Frankl further discusses that when we ask what life expects from us instead of what we expect from life, sometimes the answer is to simply accept fate, to bear our cross. So the seventh and final lesson from Tyler is to persevere, stand firm, have a back up plan.

God doesn't leave us defenseless when we face the battles of life. He gives us the tools and weapons we need. It is up to us to properly use the weapons. Tyler was very knowledgeable about weapons. Weapon was probably one of his favorite words. He loved to play the video game Dark Cloud, which requires a weapon or tool to complete each quest. He also loved learning about military weapons. So the concept of using weapons for cross-bearing was not new to Tyler. The cross of DSRCT was just so much heavier than any of us expected.

Tyler's weapons were many, but for this lesson I will limit the list to four. Two are external and two are internal.

Weapon #1 excellent healthcare, doctors, nurses and facilities

Tyler's cancer was extremely rare and therefore the treatment was still experimental, trial and error you could call it. But in spite of this, we were fortunate to live close to one of the few places in the U. S. that would give Tyler the treatment that offered the best hope for a cure.

Tyler's strong body tolerated 10 rounds of high dose chemo, 14 different chemo drugs, 5 abdominal surgeries to debulk the tumor, a stem cell transplant, numerous other procedures, scans and drugs. Throughout his 19-month battle Tyler rarely complained. He did expect high quality care from the nurses and doctors and he would not hesitate to point out problems or make suggestions on how to improve something, as any Young Marine officer would do. Sometimes the nurses appreciated his help and sometimes they didn't.

In the end, the treatment failed, but thanks to CHOC, Tyler's oncologists and surgeons, the nurses, nurse's aids, radiologists and many others, Tyler knew that he had received the most aggressive treatment for this even more aggressive cancer. Life is difficult.

Weapon #2 love and support of family and friends

While Tyler endured the very aggressive treatment, he was also a very pampered patient. He was showered daily with expression of love, kindness and support. Daily he received e-mails, cards, calls, gifts and visits. This support came from all over the country and the world including, Mexico, Canada, New Zealand, Guyana, Philippines, Saudi Arabia, Iraq and others. This support came from family, friends we knew and friends we only knew through mail or the internet. This support came from all ages, young children, teenagers, adults and senior citizens. This support came from men and women, different races, different economic status, some were wealthy most were not, some highly educated and all were educated in brotherly kindness.

Tyler and I talked about how these gifts of support seemed to come at just the right moment or place. It was amazing that someone would call or write and say just the right words needed for that moment; or a visitor would stop by and give Tyler an opportunity to discuss the news, tell a funny story, or show them his latest incision. I don't know if this was providence or just an ability to take each day's gifts and apply them as needed. Solomon said in Proverbs 25:11 *"A word aptly spoken is like apples of gold in settings of silver."* Tyler was loved and pampered, but life is difficult.

Weapon #3 perseverance, fortitude and courage

But even with this abundance of external weapons it was still up to Tyler to bear this cross, it was his destiny to have cancer, his fate to suffer. Thomas Fuller M.D. said, *What cannot be altered must be borne, not blamed."* So Tyler was faced with one of those questions of life, one of those questions of Ecclesiastes. How do I face this battle? Perseverance or despondency; courage or despair; to stand firm or flee. Tyler was 17 years old, he had faced the typical challenges of being a teenager, but his diagnosis made all of those other challenges seem very, very insignificant. Webster's defines perseverance as, "steady persistence in spite of difficulties, obstacles or discouragement." I prefer Tyler's definition, "to continue to trust God during difficult days."

Tyler chose perseverance, courage, fortitude and to stand firm. Of course, he had days of discouragement and bitter disappointment, but Tyler was a good soldier. Paul said in I Cor. 15:58, *"Therefore, stand firm, let nothing move you."* Hebrews 12:1 says, *"let us run with perseverance the race marked out for us."* Romans 5:3-4 says, *"We know that suffering produces perseverance."* And James, the brother of Jesus, wrote, *"Blessed is the man who perseveres under trial, because when he has stood the test, he will receive the crown of life"* (James 1:12).

Tyler's best hope for a cure was to reduce the cancer to microscopic disease through high dose chemo. Then have even higher dose chemo that would kill the microscopic disease, but would also destroy his bone marrow. He would then have a stem cell transplant to restore his bone marrow. In December of 2003, after one year of intense treatment, Tyler was ready for the transplant. During this 12-month period although he was in and out of the hospital frequently, we all remained hopeful that Tyler would win this battle. He talked about plans for his future, to maybe go to med school, to write a book about his experience or to just be a regular kid again and not be special anymore.

Tyler's stem cell transplant was delayed for two weeks because of a severe case of shingles. While this caused us concern, Tyler persevered and stood firm like a soldier in battle. He even maintained his sense of humor and again took pleasure in showing anyone that cared to see, the worst case of shingles most doctors have seen.

Tyler was in the hospital for 28 days for his transplant. He had some complications but to be discharged on the 28th day is very good, some patients spend months in the hospital. But our optimism soon turned to heartbreak, within a month the tumor had come back. Tyler again had surgery to debulk the tumor. He still needed transfusions every 4-5 days because his bone marrow had not recovered.

One day long before his transplant, we were watching one of Tyler's favorite movies, Forrest Gump. At one point Tyler said, "here comes my favorite line." When Jenny returns to her childhood home where she had been abused she begins to throw rocks at the old farmhouse, and then collapses. Forrest says, "Sometimes there just aren't enough rocks." I ask why that was his favorite line? Tyler answered that sometimes you just have to let things go. Tyler had run out of rocks. But he had a back up plan, as all good soldiers do. The doctors then began to talk about palliative treatment and quality of life instead of a cure. Life is difficult, but it is a gift. A gift to use and enjoy.

Weapon #4 trust in God

"I have been driven many times to my knees by the overwhelming conviction that I had nowhere else to go." Abraham Lincoln. Tyler had run out of rocks, his treatment was now palliative. Tyler hated that word. His once strong and fit body was weak and tired. As his physical body continued to suffer, his spiritual body stood

firm. Tyler had held the weapon of trust in God for a long time, but now it was his last weapon. We didn't have the answers to those questions of life. We had God's promises but not His explanations. Paul wrote in 2 Cor. 5:7, *"We live by faith, not by sight."*

Tyler questioned why he had to suffer, to bear this cross, but he found no answers. Tyler was questioned by life and he answered with perseverance, courage and trust in God. Life is a gift, treasure it!

"Now everything has been heard; here is the conclusion of the matter: Fear God and keep his commandments, for this is the whole duty of man." Ecclesiastes 12:13

Summary

So we have come full circle. Tyler's first lesson was to anchor our souls to the hope in Christ and to build a foundation through trust in God. Now we close the last lesson in the same way. By trusting in God, we prepare for death, we then are free to live a life full of learning, communicating, humor, compassion and patience. Don't fear death, prepare for it. Then when you are given the burden of suffering you can stand firm through courage.

"But there was no need to be ashamed of tears, for tears bore witness that a man had the greatest of courage, the courage to suffer." Victor Frankl

APPLICATION LESSON 7 PERSEVERANCE

Key principle: Persevere, stand firm, have a back-up plan. Life is difficult, but it is a gift, treasure it.

Verse to remember: Heb. 10:36

Psalm to read: Psalm 139

Words to study: persevere, trials, suffering, endurance

Website to visit: www.charactercounts.org

Recommended book: Man's Search for Meaning by Viktor E. Frankl

Something to do today: Write about five things you are grateful for today. Be specific.

Spring 2004 Season of Sorrow and Grief

Tyler was born in the season of summer; spring would be his last season. April and May, the last two months, were brutal. As the cancer consumed Tyler's abdomen, he endured five more surgeries to relieve the symptoms of pain and blockage of the GI tract and urinary system. He spent most of April at CHOC, but by May with all the tubes in place we were able to stay home. Our goal was to spend the little time left at home.

Tyler continued to receive and enjoy visitors, although the high dose of pain medication dulled his sharp mind. The last week, he needed someone close by at all times. Friends would stay with him during the day. Travis would read his messages and mail to him. Ken and I took turns caring for him at night. The morning of May 26th I was exhausted from being up all night and was considering having Tyler admitted to CHOC. Then God sent us an angel, the phone rang and it was my sister, Jill. She ask, "what do you need?" I said one word, "help." She replied, "I will be right there." She made the drive from Simi Valley in record time.

With her help, we kept Tyler comfortable and held his hand throughout the night while his breathing slowed and diminished. Tyler died at 4:38 am on May 27th, 2004. It was a Thursday. Soldier Boy never did get to be a Marine, but he fought like one.

Semper fi

Spring 2004 Messages to Tyler

Hello from Florida

Lindsey Ruth March 28, 2004

I love you all so much! Soldier Boy, I am glad you are feeling good right now. Maybe people will be able to put up with you now:) How is your writing going? It has been good to hear your voice on the phone, even though we did not get to talk long the other night. Yeah, yeah, I understand...you're popular. You had friends to hang out with. (At least that was your excuse for cutting our conversation short:) I miss you, and I will talk to you later this week! Have you seen Hildago? I'm throwing in my recommendation for that movie! Love you all,

Lindsey

You're Lauryn's Hero

Carol Stewart April 07, 2004

Tyler,

Lauryn was assigned to write a letter to someone who she views as a hero, and she wrote to you. It seems you made quite an impression on her that Sunday at lunch to celebrate Steve Smith's homecoming from Iraq. She said you have taught her to be a better person spiritually, and we know this is true because she is talking to us about becoming a Christian. She's on the shy side, but I think she would like share the letter with you, so watch your mail.

We continue to pray for God to watch over you and your family.

Rob, Carol & Lauryn

Hello!
Jackie Anderson April 12, 2004

Tyler,

You are a blessing from God! I admire your determination and strength. You have got quite a support group... friends, friends, friends. Wow! You have been in my daily prayers and will continue to be from now on. Good luck with this new treatment.

One of your many fans at ARB,

Love,

Jackie Anderson

Hey Tyler Teague
Geri Meraz April 14, 2004

You don't know me...........but I know you!!! Its amazing how that ripple effect works, you have no idea how you touch other people's lives. You certainly have touched my life and made a huge impact on it. I have had the pleasure........ok not all the time pleasant.....working for your father, Ken Teague. I know when I moved here to Orange County, God put me on this path. Why did he have to put me in the most expensive place to live? I have enjoyed my time with your father. The stories he has shared has been heartbreaking and full of love.........but most of all so much faith. Faith is that ripple effect. We must all feel it.....and yet we sometimes don't know where it comes from. I am so happy you have your faith. I wrote this poem based on your father and need to share it with you. Tyler Teague.........I love your name. It rhymes and sounds like a song. I pray for you and your family and friends. Love Geri

Courage

Everyday you come to your hiding place.

I absorb your mood and don't like the pain I feel.

Everyday I am amazed at your courage.

Where does that spirit come from?
I know faith is deep inside you.
I feel it from your hiding place.
True determination I have learned from you.
You cannot run from this fact......even if you had a chance.
So you sit in your hiding place.
Waiting for the future to be told.

We believe in Miracles!
Wilma Kindrick April 15, 2004
Hi Tyler,
It has been a blessing to us to see your witness. God is not through with you. He has a plan and with His help you will see it through. We are praying for that miracle of healing.
We love you.
Uncle Norman and Aunt Wilma from Texas

Hello from the Lanes
Lorraine Lane May 18, 2004
Tyler,
We're hoping that the IV gives you some strength and comfort.
Remember when you would be in your Young Marine uniform and I would tell you how, when you put your uniform on, you would do it proudly, how you would stand more erect, how you honored and respected your uniform? You would always shyly smile, thank me and go about your way. Now, when I think about you, I see that it wasn't donning your uniform that made you that way, it was you living your life that way that made the uniform seem proud and respected and honored. As your friends, that is how you make us feel. You remain in our prayers. God bless you.
Lorraine

Praying and Fasting for Tyler

Jerry Miller May 19, 2004

Dear Tyler

Just wanted to let you know how much you mean to us. I want to say thanks for you being you. I want to say thanks to your mom and dad for letting you stay with us for a while. Do you remember working on the cotton stripper? Or how about when my new yellow boll buggy was delivered and you were helping by running the fork-lift while we changed out the axles. Anyway, I remember it. And every time I'm around a stripper I think of you. Or how about working on the preacher's floor. Those are good memories we made together. I want to say thanks for fighting this cancer so hard. Never has any Marine had to fight such a tough battle. Never has a Marine shown his true metal, true courage, his true strength. No one could have fought this battle as you have.

We love you much,

Jerry, Arlene and kids

Strength

Leslie Flad May 20, 2004

Tyler, Ken and Judy - It's hard to find the right words to say. We have been following your progress and praying very faithfully for the last year. Now that we know you will be in heaven because of your faith in our God, all we can say now is ... we'll see you there. We will all miss you here on earth, but you have such a special mansion prepared for you there that you will get to enjoy it much sooner than us. Our prayer now is that you will not be in pain and that those surrounding you will absorb every minute they can of you and that they will treasure those moments till their time comes. Our prayers, thoughts, hearts and emotions are with you now.

Love in Him, The Flads

Great Seeing You All
Randy Hilburn May 20, 2004

I know it was only a couple of hours, but Judy and I were so grateful to be able to spend some time with you. With Tyler's care being a non-stop operation, we were thankful that you made the time to be so kind and so hospitable. All this morning, I couldn't stop thinking about how a "death in the Lord" crystallizes the depth of meaning in these meager lives we live. Maybe it's even more significant when someone isn't able to live out his "dreams." In the end, no matter how long our trip is down here, only one "career goal/dream" has any substance. Thank you, Lord, for giving sense to our pain. Thank you, Tyler, for allowing us to sit in "your" classroom. I always thought you were among the most thoughtful of the students in those Jr. High Bible Classes. Little did we know that you were preparing to teach the most important lesson of them all.

We love you. Judy and Randy

Sweet Tyler
Kristi Elsom May 21, 2004

Dear Tyler

May the Lord richly bless the time you spend with those who love you, and may the thoughts and prayers of those of us who can not be there in person comfort you and your family. You have touched so many lives during your time on earth with your laugh, your smile, and your witness for God. You have made a difference! Thank you for making our world better.

I love you my dear brother in Christ,

Kristi

No Tears in Heaven
Jane Hensley May 27, 2004
As the tears of sorrow are flowing down here on earth, we know that Tyler will no longer be hurting and there are no tears in heaven. He has gone home to the Father. Our prayers continue to be lifted up to you in this time of physical loss. May you find comfort in God's loving arms during this time.
Jane Sneed Hensley

Expression of sympathy.
Colin MacDonald May 27, 2004
To the Teague Family;
Please accept my deepest sympathy on your loss. Tyler has been an inspiration for all that have shared his journey - a true warrior in his long battle. May the strength you have shown as a family assist you through this difficult time.
Colin MacDonald
Port Hawkesbury, Nova Scotia

From a speechless friend
Keith Houchin May 27, 2004
My condolences and sympathies to the entire Teague family and everyone else who knew Tyler as I did. I know nothing to say that will fit this message other than see you on the flip side. Rest in peace my friend.

-Keith Houchin

Song of My Life

The Question
The answer on the tip of everyone's tongue
Never in the air
It's not important
It cannot control lives unless it is allowed
The wind, the rain, and the sun
They are part of the question
The body, mind, and soul
They are part of the question
Whether one searches for the answer
Or lets it wash over them
Happiness or sadness may come
Happiness is far sweeter then sadness
I chose happiness
With questioning in the mind
And happiness in the heart
The day begins
The question never answered leads to more
Does the question have a universal answer?
Should one even be looking?

Is it possible to understand?
Have we encased the answer in concrete?
Friends will answer with
Speculation
Stop questioning
Look at the sky
Feel the beauty
Feel the sun's warmth
Breathe the air
Feel happiness
Sadness
Fright
Pain
Awareness
And you will not question
The answer is not there
But it will not matter
Because you will have lived
The answer

Tyler Teague (May 2002)

Source Notes

Man's Search for Meaning by Viktor E. Frankl, Beacon Press, 1992.

The Simpsons: A complete guide to our favorite family by Matt Groening, HarperCollins 1997.

The Simpsons and Philosophy: The D'oh! of Homer edited by William Irwin, Mark T. Conard, and Aeon J. Skoble, Open Court 2001.

Mere Christianity by C. S. Lewis, HarperCollins 2001.

Philosophy for Dummies by Tom Morris, Ph.D., Wiley Publishing, Inc. 1999.

Life's Greatest Lessons by Hal Urban, Simon and Schuster 2003.

Printed in the United States
40045LVS00006B/448-531